THE 10-DAY SELF-DISCIPLINE CHALLENGE

A PROVEN PATH TO SUCCESS: MASTER YOUR MIND IN JUST 10 DAYS WITH REWARDING 5-MINUTE EXERCISES TO CREATE GOOD HABITS AND ACHIEVE YOUR GOALS

C. L. VALENTE

CONTENTS

INTRODUCTION

Are you tired of feeling like you lack control over your life? Do you struggle to stick to your goals and create lasting habits? If so, you're not alone. Many of us have experienced the frustration of setting ambitious goals, only to fall short due to a lack of discipline. The promises we make to ourselves and the goals we set often dissolve in the face of daily distractions and temptations. But what if there was a way to break free from this cycle? What if I tell you that in just 10 days you could gain the self-discipline necessary to take charge of your life and achieve your dreams?

Welcome to *The 10-Day Self-Discipline Challenge: A Proven Path to Success – Master Your Mind in Just 10 Days With Rewarding 5-Minute Exercises to Create Good Habits and Achieve Your Goals.* By choosing to embark on this journey, you've taken a crucial step toward a more disciplined and fulfilling life. This isn't just another pack of self-help theories that don't work; it's a practical guide filled with actionable strategies, effective tips, and exercises that have been proven to work repeatedly.

You might be wondering why self-discipline matters. It's more than just a trait; it's the secret sauce that helps you achieve your life goals—big or small. Whether you aim to write a book, get in shape, or start your own business, self-discipline will turn your long-nurtured dream into a reality. It's about making conscious choices that align with your long-term goals, even when Netflix and social media are calling.

I want you to think of self-discipline as a muscle. The more you work on it, the stronger it gets (and that's what we'll be doing in this book). Imagine waking up each morning with a clear sense of purpose and direction. Instead of feeling overwhelmed by the tasks ahead, you approach them with confidence and determination. That's the power of self-discipline—it empowers you to make consistent progress toward your goals, no matter how big or small.

Okay, confession time. Like many of you, I've faced my battles with self-discipline. Sometimes I struggled to focus on my priorities and found myself easily distracted from my goals. Procrastination became my best friend, and my goals seemed to drift farther away. However, from a very young age, my mantra has been "Practice doesn't make perfect but does make better, and anything worth having is worth working for. Seldom is anything handed to you on a plate." I was once drowned in the ocean of procrastination and lack of self-motivation but never self-doubt simply because I believed everything I wanted was ultimately down to me.

Over the years, I've studied and practiced tips, tricks, and exercises to help me stay on track—something I've shared with many over time. Whether it be sticking to a healthy diet, taking exercise, dealing with business matters, or making time for family and friends, none of these challenges are unconquerable. Yet, we often view them as mountain tasks that are impossible to accomplish.

Through my years of building self-discipline, I learned a great lesson: My small wins give me satisfaction, and a sense of achievement, put a smile on my face, a bounce in my step, and give me the confidence to carry on even when I want to give up. These small victories—whether it was resisting that extra slice of cake, completing a workout, or finishing a task ahead of time—provided the motivation I needed to keep pushing forward. They taught me self-discipline isn't about making huge leaps but taking small, consistent steps toward your goals. Each step, no matter how tiny, builds up your confidence and resilience. My dream now is to help as many people as I can with their self-discipline struggles so they can experience a more fulfilling and happy life. I'm really excited you're one of those joining me on this journey. By sharing what I've learned over the years, I hope to guide you toward the same sense of achievement and joy that comes from mastering self-discipline.

In *The 10-Day Self-Discipline Challenge*, I'm sharing with you the very strategies and exercises that have made a profound impact on my life. These aren't just random tips from a self-proclaimed guru. They're practical tools designed to fit into your busy life. Each day of this challenge will introduce you to new concepts and exercises that are easy to implement, even if you've got a schedule crazier than a cat herder in a thunderstorm.

From mindfulness practices that take just five minutes a day to productivity hacks that actually work, you're about to open a hidden treasure chest full of resources to support your journey toward greater self-discipline.

Over the next 10 days, get ready to embark on a journey of self-discovery and personal growth. Each day will focus on a different aspect of self-discipline, guiding you through exercises that will challenge your mindset and habits. You'll learn how to overcome procrastination, stay motivated when life throws you a curveball, and build habits that set you up for success.

Day 1 kicks off with laying the foundation—understanding what self-discipline truly means for you, how it differs from motivation, and some common misconceptions about self-discipline. From there, each day builds upon the last, introducing practical tips and reflections that encourage introspection and action.

By Day 3, you might start feeling the initial resistance—this is perfectly normal. Change is always challenging at first. But stick with it! You'll find that by tackling one small issue each day, the bigger picture starts to come together.

Around Day 5, things begin to click. You'll notice how the little shifts in your behavior and mindset are starting to compound. Maybe you're finding it easier to get out of bed in the morning or to say "no" to binge-watching Netflix. These seemingly small victories are actually huge steps toward building long-lasting self-discipline.

By the end of this challenge, expect to see some serious changes. We're talking about improvements in your ability to stay focused, set meaningful goals, and follow through like a pro. The lessons you learn and the habits you develop will be your secret sauce for future achievements, whether it's acing that project at work or finally fitting into those jeans you've been eyeing.

I know you might be wondering, why 10 days? The idea behind this timeframe is to kickstart your journey toward self-discipline with a manageable, yet impactful, commitment. Ten days is short enough to feel achievable, but long enough to begin forming new habits. It's like planting a seed and watching it sprout—these 10 days will give you the initial push you need to continue growing and thriving long after the challenge is over. So, the push doesn't end in 10 days!

Each day's tasks are designed to be simple and quick. We're talking about five-minute tasks that fit into even the busiest of schedules. The goal is to make self-discipline accessible and not overwhelming. From overcoming procrastination to slowly building self-control, these activities are small but mighty. They're crafted to bring about big changes without requiring a huge time investment.

And let's make one thing clear: This challenge isn't about making your life harder or adding stress. It's about enhancing your life, making it more fulfilling and enjoyable. Self-discipline doesn't have to be all serious and stern. In fact, the more fun it is, the more easier it is! Think of the tips shared in this book as little games or personal experiments. You're exploring what works best for you and finding joy in the process of self-improvement.

So, are you ready to take control of your life and unlock your full potential? Turn the page and get started on this transformative journey. The next 10 days will challenge you, inspire you, and ultimately empower you to become the best version of yourself. Your future self is waiting—let's embark on this adventure together.

Remember, this is your journey and if you do it the right way, your future self will thank you. Take it at your own pace, celebrate your progress, and don't be too hard on yourself if you stumble. Every step you take is a step toward a better, more disciplined you. Let's dive in and start this exciting adventure together!

CHAPTER 1
UNDERSTANDING SELF-DISCIPLINE

Success is not the result of spontaneous combustion. You must set yourself on fire.

ARNOLD H. GLASGOW

Understanding self-discipline is important, so bear with me as we discuss this critical aspect.

Imagine you're trying to build a house. You have the vision, the blueprints, and all the necessary materials. While all these form an essential part of your plan, without a strong foundation, your house will eventually crumble. Self-discipline is that foundation. It's the steady, reliable base upon which all your efforts and aspirations rest. Without it, even the most brilliant plans can fall.

Self-discipline is often seen as a stern and joyless taskmaster, but in reality, it's quite the opposite. Think of it as your best friend who always looks out for you, guiding you away from distractions and keeping you focused on what truly matters. It's the quiet force that helps you push through challenges and stay committed to your goals, even when motivation wanes.

However, there are many misconceptions about self-discipline. It's often portrayed as an innate trait that some people just have, and others don't. But this couldn't be further from the truth. Self-discipline is a skill anyone can develop with practice and the right strategies. It's also commonly mistaken for sheer willpower, but in reality, it's much more than just forcing yourself to do things you don't want to do.

In this chapter, we'll dive deep into the importance of self-discipline, differentiate between self-discipline and motivation, explore the science behind it, and debunk some common myths. By the end, you'll understand how to harness this powerful tool to achieve your goals and improve your life. So, let's set that steady flame of self-discipline alight and embark on this journey together.

THE IMPORTANCE OF SELF-DISCIPLINE

Discipline generally encompasses training individuals to adhere to certain rules or ways of doing things. Self-discipline isn't far different from this. It's the inward effort to control and train our minds, behavior, and body.

Simply, we can define self-discipline as the ability to stay motivated, push yourself, and take action irrespective of how you feel physically or emotionally. It's not tearing yourself down or having no self-compassion; instead, it's intentionally pursuing what's better for your life despite distractions, unfavorable odds, and temptations. Self-discipline is when you can control yourself and do things in a particular way without needing someone else to tell or push you.

Self-Discipline as the Cornerstone of Success

Self-discipline is a very important and needed skill in everyone's life. It's that force that propels you toward success in all aspects of life. Here are some benefits of self-discipline:

Increased Productivity: Self-discipline helps you stay focused. It fights off distraction and procrastination—the two major enemies of productivity. Think about how easy it is to get distracted by social media or television or idle around when you have a heap of tasks waiting for you. Self-discipline helps you combat these distractions and stay focused on your tasks, thus getting more done in less time.

It also helps you push through the tendency to procrastinate tasks you don't like or seem hard. It pushes you to start your tasks right away instead of leaving them till the last minute. This doesn't only increase your productivity but also reduces the stress of having a lot of unfinished work on your table. By developing self-discipline, you're no longer going to juggle multiple tasks without a clear plan or focus, instead, you'll have a to-do list and a clear schedule to stick to.

Achieving Goals: Another area where self-discipline shines is achieving goals. It's the driving force that inspires you to set and achieve your goals. It helps you to stay focused on your objectives, reminding you of why you set them in the first place. Self-discipline also enables you to manage time effectively, ensuring you create a schedule that prioritizes your goals and dedicate time each day to work toward them. It also equips you to handle the challenges and setbacks that come with achieving your goals. Self-discipline is what propels you forward, even when things become challenging.

Enhancing Personal Responsibility: Cultivating self-discipline helps boost your sense of self-responsibility. It teaches you to own up to your actions and their outcomes. This sense of responsibility pushes you to make choices more aligned with your values and long-term goals, not just what makes you feel good now. It makes you hold yourself accountable not only in your commitments to others but also in commitments to yourself, thus changing the way you handle things, from day-to-day tasks to major life decisions.

Achieving Personal Growth: Self-discipline is like your personal trainer who pushes you out of your comfort zone and nudges you to push your limits and get better at what you do. It's a key ingredient in learning new skills or tackling tough challenges. Look at it like learning to play the guitar; at the beginning, it gives you sore fingers and not much better sounds, but with persistence and constant practice, you'll start to make actual music. Before you know it, you'll become a pro and start playing whole songs. That's growth, and it comes from sticking to it, even when it's tempting to skip a day or give up when it feels too hard.

Improved Self-Confidence: Self-discipline does wonders in boosting our self-worth and confidence. When you stick to your plans and hit your goals, it's like giving yourself a high five. Each little win builds your confidence bit by bit and tells you, "Hey, you can do this!" The sense of accomplishment pumps up your self-esteem and makes you proud. Don't forget: The better you feel about yourself, the more motivated you'll be to keep going and smashing those goals!

How Self-Discipline Differs From Motivation

When did you last feel motivated after watching a video, listening to a podcast, or reading a book? These types of things certainly motivate me. Did you get a rush and start racing toward a new goal? Did you keep pushing till you achieved that goal, or did you eventually fall off along the way? Here's where motivation differs from self-discipline.

While many view self-discipline and motivation as the same, the two are quite different. We can agree they're on the same team, but each plays a different role. Motivation is the initial burst of energy you get when you develop a new idea or set a new goal. It's that energy pump to start a new diet after watching an inspiring weight loss video.

However, motivation is a bit tricky because it's driven by emotions that come and go. This hour, you feel on top of the world, ready to start a fitness journey or learn a new course, and the next, you're just curling up on the couch, scrolling social media aimlessly.

That's where self-discipline steps in. It's that inner stronger and quieter push that doesn't rely on your high feelings. It's what keeps you going even after the excitement has faded away. Self-discipline is like a reliable friend that gently nudges you to go to the gym even when you don't feel like going or choose a healthy diet over fast foods due to your long-term health goals.

While self-discipline is what makes you accomplish your goals, motivation is what drives you to exceed expectations. With self-discipline alone, if you take all the needed steps, you'll be able to reach your goals, but motivation is like a friend who takes your hand and encourages you to go the extra mile.

For example, after the initial thrill (motivation) of starting a diet wears off, self-discipline makes you choose healthy meals when you'd rather have pizza. Or when you're learning a language, it's the thing that makes you practice your vocabulary every day, even when you don't feel like it.

In essence, motivation is what gets you started, but self-discipline is what keeps you on the path. It's about making consistent choices that align with your long-term goals, not just when it feels exciting. That steady commitment that comes from self-discipline is what brings about success and helps you grow.

The Psychological Benefits of Self-Discipline

Self-discipline has important and transformative psychological benefits that greatly shape how we feel about ourselves and manage our daily lives. Here are some of these benefits in detail:

Reduced Stress Levels: Self-discipline plays an essential role in reducing stress by bringing order to your day. When you have solid control over your routines and habits, you won't have the last-minute rush that can result in chaos which often leads to increased stress levels. It's so much better starting the day knowing exactly what tasks to do, from the moment you wake up to when you retire to bed. This organized approach prevents the anxiety of struggling at work or submitting tasks after deadlines. By being consistent with your daily routine, you'll remain organized and finish all tasks ahead of the deadline, thus ensuring a less stressful and smoother daily experience.

Enhanced Self-Esteem and Self-Efficacy: A rewarding psychological benefit of self-discipline is boosting self-esteem and self-efficacy. Every time you achieve something through self-discipline, it's like sending a good message to yourself about your worth and abilities. This success boosts your self-esteem, making you feel more capable and competent. Also, your self-efficacy—the belief in your ability to achieve your goals—grows, and you become more ready to take on new challenges and push your boundaries. This cycle of positive reinforcement makes you feel stronger and more empowered to face life and chase success.

Improved Mental Health: Self-discipline is the foundation of self-control and self-care. When disciplined, you prioritize your well-being and engage in activities that enhance your mental health. These include consistent routines in eating a healthy diet, exercising, getting enough sleep, and practicing mindfulness that not only improves your physical state but also significantly improves your psychological state.

Also, self-discipline provides you with a high level of self-control, which is essential for managing behaviors and emotions. Through self-control, you can avoid impulsive behaviors that may affect your mental health in the long run. It also helps you to resist the temptation of falling into bad habits or addictions.

Greater Perseverance: Another significant psychological benefit of self-discipline is the development of unmatched resilience and perseverance. With strong self-discipline, you'll always be ready to bounce back after setbacks and face life challenges without being easily overwhelmed. Each time your self-discipline helps you to overcome an obstacle, you not only solve the immediate problem but also build up your resilience muscle, meaning you're more equipped to handle future stress and setbacks. Resilience is what gives individuals the ability to not lose momentum after experiencing failure or setbacks. Instead, you analyze what went wrong, adjust your strategies, and move forward stronger and fortified by your self-discipline.

Overall, self-discipline enriches your psychological well-being in many ways, making it an essential trait in managing stress, enhancing self-efficacy, caring for your mental health, and building perseverance.

THE SCIENCE BEHIND SELF-DISCIPLINE

Self-discipline isn't just about forcing yourself to do things you don't want. There's a lot of interesting science behind it, which can help us understand why it works and how to get better at it. Let's look at how our brain plays a role in self-control and self-discipline.

Exploring the Brain's Role in Self-Control

The brain has a special part called the prefrontal cortex, which acts as the control center for making decisions, planning, and focusing. It's the part of the brain that evolved most recently, and when things are going well, it acts as the control center that keeps our impulses and baser emotions in check (Arnsten et al., 2012).

The prefrontal cortex is the most highly evolved brain region, larger proportionally in humans than in other primates, and occupies ⅓ of the human cortex. It matures slowly and attains full maturity after teen years. The prefrontal cortex is responsible for performing "executive functions" like problem-solving, resulting in emotions and controlling impulses. It helps the brain to keep everything organized and on track. When the prefrontal cortex is strong and well-developed, it becomes easier to stay disciplined.

Research has shown that dieters who successfully turn down unhealthy food temptations put more emphasis on the healthiness of the food and less on its taste. This is the opposite of dieters who can't say "no" to sweet foods. Despite trying to eat a healthier diet, they cannot shift away from the stronger representation of taste. Using functional magnetic resonance imaging (FMRI), scientists were able to see how the ventral medial prefrontal cortex becomes active in making choices like this. This area of the brain has also been shown to be involved in some monetary decisions—for example, when researchers present subjects with the option of getting a larger reward later or a smaller one immediately. The scientists also located a second important brain area—the dorsolateral frontal cortex—which is more active when participants choose options that appear better to them in the long run—for instance, healthy food or a larger reward later. The study shows that the interaction between these brain regions—the ventral medial frontal cortex and the dorsolateral frontal cortex—is stronger in people with higher self-control (Hare et al., 2009).

The more you use your self-control, the stronger your prefrontal cortex becomes, like a muscle. So, every time you choose to study instead of binge-watching Netflix or go for veggies instead of fries, you're giving your prefrontal cortex a workout, making it better at helping you stay disciplined in the future.

The Impact of Self-Discipline on Neuroplasticity

Neuroplasticity, also known as brain plasticity, is the ability of the neural network of the brain to develop through reorganization and growth. Simply saying, our brains can change and adapt based on our actions. When you practice self-discipline, you're not only making positive life choices but also reshaping the neural pathways in your brain.

Each time you resist a bad habit or practice a good habit, you create and strengthen new neural pathways. Think of it like creating a path in a forest—at first, it's all grassy, but the more you walk the path, the clearer and easier it becomes to follow.

If you've learned to play an instrument or ride a bike, you've experienced neuroplasticity. In the beginning, it's hard, and you have to focus a lot. But as you practice more and more, the brain rewires itself and becomes adaptable to such things you're learning. The case is the same with self-discipline; the more you practice, the more your brain rewires to support and carry out disciplined behaviors without much hassle. So if you keep practicing self-discipline, over time, it will become your natural way of life and less of a forced thing. Your brain will get used to the new habits and start to prefer them, making it easier for you to stick to them without fighting so hard against temptations and distractions.

Understanding the Concept of Delayed Gratification

Delayed gratification or deterred gratification is the act of resisting the temptation of an immediate reward in the hope of getting a more valued reward in the long term. It's associated with resisting smaller but immediate rewards for larger, more valuable rewards later.

A popular delayed gratification study is the Marshmallow Test carried out by American psychologist Walter Mischel and his colleagues, in which a child is asked to choose between a bigger treat, such as two marshmallows, and a smaller treat, such as one marshmallow. After choosing the larger treat, the child will learn that to get that, they have to wait for the experimenter to come back. The child is also told that if at any time they signal, the experimenter will return, and the child gets the smaller treat. Thus, the smaller treat is available now, but the larger one requires waiting (Conti, 2019).

You might be wondering why it is so hard to wait. The uncertainty about future rewards makes delayed gratification hard. We don't know when these long-term rewards will come if they come at all. Also, delayed gratification is affected by factors such as personality, social circumstances, mental health, and worldview.

For adolescents and young adults, delayed gratification is more challenging as the reward processing and impulse control centers of the brain are still developing and yet to mature fully.

Some tips that might help you improve your delayed gratification ability are:

- **Setting Definitive Timeframes:** Provide yourself with feedback on how long you need to wait before you get the bigger reward. For example, if you want to save $2000 for a vacation, set a definitive timeframe; you'll do that for six months or a year. Also, check your progress now and then to give yourself the satisfaction that you're gradually getting closer to the bigger reward.
- **Setting Realistic Deadlines:** One thing that makes delayed gratification hard for people is setting unrealistic deadlines. For example, someone trying to get in shape might vow not to eat fast food for a year. This is like setting yourself up for failure. A more realistic way to do this is to resist fast foods all week round but have a treat of your best pizza on Sunday evening.
- **Small Rewards:** Break down your larger goals into milestones and reward yourself for each. For example, if

you're saving $2000 for a vacation, break it into 4 milestones, each of $500. Reward yourself each time you reach a milestone. This keeps you motivated and makes the larger goal seem more attainable.

How Self-Discipline Impacts Behavior and Decision-Making

Self-discipline plays a great role in how we behave and make everyday decisions. With a strong sense of self-discipline, you're better at thinking about the consequences of your actions and making decisions for your betterment in the long run.

Let's say you have a big project due at work. Without self-discipline, it's easy to procrastinate and leave everything to the last minute. But with self-discipline, you can break the project into smaller tasks, set deadlines for each, and work on it steadily. This way, you avoid the stress of rushing, and you're likely to do a better job.

Self-discipline helps you prioritize what's important. Instead of acting on impulse, you take a moment to consider, "Is this the best choice for me right now?" For instance, if you're trying to save money, self-discipline helps you avoid impulse buys and stick to your budget. It might mean cooking at home instead of eating out, knowing that these small choices add to bigger savings.

Another example is health and fitness. Without self-discipline, it's easy to skip workouts or indulge in unhealthy foods. But with self-discipline, you're more likely to stick to a regular exercise routine and make healthier food choices. This doesn't mean you never have treats, but you balance them with healthy habits.

Self-discipline also helps you build better habits. When you consistently choose to act disciplined, these actions become habits. Over time, you don't have to think hard about making the right choice—it becomes automatic. This makes it easier to maintain positive behaviors and avoid negative ones.

COMMON MISCONCEPTIONS ABOUT SELF-DISCIPLINE

Self-discipline is often misunderstood. Let's clear up the common misconceptions and have a better grasp of what it means.

Debunking Myths About Willpower

Many people view self-discipline as having a ton of willpower. They think of it as gritting your teeth and forcing yourself to do things you hate. That isn't a very good picture.

Willpower is just a part of self-discipline. It's the ability to resist short-term temptations and delay gratifications to achieve long-term goals. It's the ability to override unwanted feelings and impulses and also use the "cool" cognitive system rather than the "hot" emotional system. But then, willpower is also a limited resource capable of being depleted (American Psychological Association, 2012).

In self-discipline, you control your actions to achieve a certain outcome. It involves making a conscious decision to follow a specific plan, even if it's hard to do. Willpower, on the other hand, is resisting short-term temptations or impulses to achieve a bigger goal later. Think of willpower as a muscle that can get tired if you overuse it. Self-discipline is creating habits and routines that become second nature over time.

Many see willpower as something that you either have or you don't. This isn't correct; everyone can strengthen their willpower with practice. Start small by setting manageable goals and gradually build up your self-control. Develop willpower together with self-discipline, as willpower can become harder over time as you become more stressed, while self-discipline will become ingrained in you over time.

Overcoming the Fear of Failure and Perfectionism

Another big misconception is that self-discipline means being perfect all the time. This is far from true. In reality, self-discipline isn't about perfection but rather persistence. It's about getting back on the track after you slip up. Everyone makes mistakes; what's important is how you react to them.

Many people have high expectations for how they want things to turn out, so they let the fear of failure stop them from trying. They think if it can't be done perfectly, then it's not worth doing at all. This mindset serves as a huge barrier to success and progress. Instead of trying to be perfect, focus on being consistent. If you miss a workout or break your diet, don't give up; bounce back harder and move forward.

Think of this as learning to ride a bike. You'll surely fall off sometimes, but each time you get up and ride again, you're getting better at balancing. The same goes for self-discipline; each time you recover from an obstacle, you're strengthening your ability to stay on track in the future. Remember that perfection is hardly attainable, but persistence is powerful and realistic.

Some tips to help you get over the fear of failure include:

- Accept failure as normal, and it can be part of achieving success.
- When you're worried about a situation, give yourself more options.
- Remember the cost of not trying: missing 100% of the shots you don't take!
- If you try something that doesn't turn out as expected, make a change.

Accept setbacks as part of the process and an opportunity to learn and grow rather than fail. This way, you'll overcome the fear of failure and the pressure of perfectionism while building resilience to keep working toward your goal.

Recognizing the Role of Environment in Fostering Self-Discipline

People often overlook how much their environment affects their self-discipline. Your surroundings can either make your goals easier or harder to achieve. For instance, if you're trying to cut down on screen time, but your living room is centered around the TV, it will be tough. Changing your environment plays a great role in supporting your goals.

This might mean creating a dedicated workspace to avoid distractions if you're trying to be more productive. Set up a clean, organized desk away from the TV and other distractions. Have all your work materials handy to dive into tasks without wasting time searching for things. A clutter-free, dedicated workspace can significantly boost your productivity and focus.

If your goal is to eat healthier, and your kitchen is filled with unhealthy snacks, it's hard to resist the temptation not to eat. However, if you stock your kitchen with nutritious foods, get rid of junk food or store it out of sight, and keep fruits, vegetables, and other healthy snacks easily accessible, you'll likely stick to your dietary goals.

Your social circle plays a great role in influencing your habits and behaviors. Surrounding yourself with disciplined people will naturally motivate and push you to become more self-disciplined.

Even small changes in your environment can make a big difference. For instance, if you want to read more, keep a book by your bedside table instead of your phone. This makes it easier to reach for a book instead of scrolling through social media before bed. Setting up visual cues and removing temptations can greatly enhance your ability to stay disciplined.

KEY TAKEAWAYS

- Wrapping up this chapter, we've understood that self-discipline isn't just a desirable trait but a cornerstone of personal and professional success.
- It helps boost our productivity, helps us achieve our goals, and builds self-confidence.
- It's not about being perfect but being committed and bouncing back after facing setbacks.
- It's not about being a willpower superhero or battling against your environment; instead, it's being kind to yourself and shaping your environment to make your goals easier.

In the next chapter, we'll discuss how to set clear goals, overcome barriers, and cultivate resilience in the face of setbacks. Get ready to become a pro in setting and achieving goals!

CHAPTER 2
SETTING CLEAR GOALS

Without goals and plans to reach them, you are like a ship that has set sail with no destination.

FITZHUGH DODSON

We throw around the word "goals" a lot these days. So much so that we need to figure out what a goal is. Goals are like the destination of your journey. Without them, you're just drifting along with no clear direction. But with well-defined and clear goals, you know where you're headed and how to get there.

This chapter will equip you with the right strategy for setting clear, practical goals. First, we'll discuss why being specific about what you want is essential. Vague goals like "I want to lose weight" aren't effective. Instead, your goals need to be clear and detailed. We'll introduce you to SMART goals, which are Specific, Measurable, Achievable, Relevant, and Time-Bound—super clear and realistic goals.

Once we get our goals in the bag, the next step is to plan how to achieve them. We'll talk about how to prioritize tasks and set deadlines to help you stay focused and on schedule. We'll also share tips for overcoming obstacles because, let's face it, things don't always go smoothly.

Moreover, we'll tackle common roadblocks like procrastination and self-doubt. Lastly, we'll emphasize the importance of keeping yourself accountable.

I can't emphasize enough the importance of setting clear, specific, and achievable goals; it will be a recurring theme throughout this book. Establishing well-defined goals is crucial because it provides direction and motivation, helping you stay focused and committed. As we discuss various strategies, the central role of goal-setting will become evident in overcoming challenges and maintaining progress.

By integrating these elements into your journey, you'll be better equipped to navigate obstacles and sustain your momentum.

THE POWER OF GOAL SETTING

Goals are fundamental for success in both professional and personal life. Establishing goals is an essential habit for succeeding in all spheres of life. They provide a sense of motivation, direction, and purpose, providing a roadmap that directs you to your intended results and enables you to track your development.

A study has shown that those who set specific and challenging goals have higher chances of achieving high performance compared to those who didn't set goals. Setting the right goals in the right way is the first step to success (Locke et al., 1981). But how can you set the right goals? That's what this section will guide you on.

The Importance of Clarity and Specificity in Goal Setting

Your goals are like a road map for a journey. Without a clear destination, getting lost or ending up somewhere you don't intend to be is inevitable. This is why clarity and specificity are crucial when setting goals. These two characteristics work together to accelerate your progress in your growth and development journey.

Clarity in goal setting means understanding exactly what you want and how to achieve it. The clearer you are about your goal, the more consistent and motivated you will be. This clarity enables you to pinpoint your priorities and tailor your schedules accordingly.

Specificity includes breaking down your goals into detailed steps. Specific goals eliminate ambiguity and enable you to track your progress. When your goals are specific, you can divide them into smaller and more manageable segments, which helps you remain motivated and make necessary adjustments.

Clear and specific goals are beneficial for several reasons:

1. **Enhanced Focus:** When you have a clear and specific goal, it's easier to focus your efforts. You know exactly what you're working toward, so you can prioritize your tasks and allocate your resources more effectively.
2. **Improved Motivation:** Clear goals are motivating because they provide a tangible outcome for which to strive. Specific goals also make it easier to celebrate milestones along the way, boosting your morale and keeping you engaged.
3. **Better Planning:** Specific goals allow for detailed planning. When you know what you want to achieve and when you can create a step-by-step plan to reach your goal, this plan can include smaller tasks and deadlines, making the overall goal less overwhelming and more manageable.

4. **Easier Measurement of Progress:** Clear and specific goals provide a way to measure your progress. You can track how far you've come and see how close you are to achieving your goal.

5. **Greater Resilience:** You're better prepared to handle setbacks when your goals are clear and specific. You can quickly identify what's not working and adjust your plan accordingly.

Setting SMART Goals for Maximum Effectiveness

Setting goals is essential, but making sure they're SMART goals takes it further. SMART stands for **S**pecific, **M**easurable, **A**chievable, **R**elevant, and **T**ime-Bound. SMART goals are practical because they provide structure and clarity. They help you focus on what's important, eliminate distractions, and maintain motivation over time.

1. **Specific:** Your goals need to be specific and clear. To make your goal specific, ask yourself: *Who's involved in the goal? What do I want to achieve? Where can I achieve it? When can I achieve it? And why do I want to achieve it?* For example, instead of saying, "I want to be healthier," be specific: "I want to lose 10 pounds in three months by exercising five times a week and eating a balanced diet." This clarity helps you focus your efforts and understand precisely what you must do.

2. **Measurable:** A goal without criteria for measuring progress is like a sports game without a scoreboard. Measurability lets you track your progress and know whether you're on track. A measurable goal must be able to answer these questions: *How many? How do I know I've reached where I want to be? And what is the indicator of my progress?* For instance, "I want to save $5,000 for a vacation in a year, and I'll do that by cutting off unnecessary expenses" gives you a specific amount to aim for and a timeframe to achieve it.

3. **Achievable:** Your goal needs to be realistic and attainable. While setting goals that will stretch your abilities is essential, you should set what's possible for you. Setting a goal to run a marathon next month when you've never run before isn't achievable. Instead, set a goal to run a 5K in three months, gradually building up your endurance. This way, you've set a challenging yet achievable goal.

4. **Relevant:** Goals should align with your overarching objectives and values. If your goal is relevant, it will matter to you and fit within your overall plan. When you set goals, every action you take should move you a step closer to achieving that goal. For example, if your long-term career goal is to become a project manager, a relevant short-term goal might be completing a project management certification course.

5. **Time-Bound:** every goal needs a deadline to create a sense of urgency and provide a clear target date for completion. Having a deadline keeps you focused on what you're working toward. It's also essential to determine whether your goal is short-term or long-term. A time-bound goal might be, "I want to finish writing my book by the end of the year." This deadline helps you pace your work and stay focused on the result.

Examples of SMART Goals

Let's look at a couple of examples to see how goals can be turned into SMART goals:

1. Non-SMART goal: "I want to learn a new language."

SMART goal: "I will complete a beginner's course in Spanish within six months by studying for 30 minutes every day."

2. Non-SMART goal: "I want to be more productive at work."

SMART goal: "I will improve my productivity by using task management tools to prioritize my tasks and complete all high-priority tasks by the end of each day for the next three months."

3. Non-SMART goal: "I want to save money."

SMART goal: "I will save $1,000 in six months by setting aside $50 from my paycheck weekly and cutting back on dining out to twice a month."

4. Non-SMART goal: "I want to improve my public speaking skills."

SMART goal: "I will enhance my public speaking skills by joining a local public speaking club and delivering at least one speech per month, aiming to complete six speeches in six months."

These examples show how turning vague aspirations into SMART goals gives you a clear plan and timeline, making it easier to stay focused and achieve your objectives.

Visualizing Success and Creating a Roadmap to Achievement

Visualization is a technique where you imagine yourself thriving in your goals. It's like a mental rehearsal that prepares your mind for success. This isn't daydreaming; instead, creating a vivid picture of your success boosts your confidence and motivates you. By vividly imagining your desired outcomes, you'll set clear directions to work toward achieving your goals. For example, if you're aiming to excel in your business, through visualization, you'll be able to see yourself pitching ideas, meeting with potential partners, and landing big deals. This visualization provides a sense of familiarity and makes it easier to navigate obstacles and make decisions that will push you toward success.

Creating your roadmap involves breaking down larger goals into smaller and more manageable ones. This approach makes the task less daunting and helps you stay more focused. To create your roadmap, start with a clear and specific goal, which you'll break into several major milestones that will mark significant progress along your journey. For each milestone, outline actions you need to take—these are your action steps, which must also be clear and specific.

For instance, to achieve the milestone of completing a course, your action steps will include researching relevant courses, enrolling in the one you think best fits you, and setting aside time to study every day. Another thing to include in your roadmap to success is potential challenges that could arise and the best way to tackle them.

CREATING AN ACTION PLAN

Setting goals is a great start, but turning those goals into reality requires a solid action plan. An action plan is like a detailed map that guides you step by step toward achieving your goals. It breaks down your bigger objectives into smaller, manageable tasks and sets a clear path forward. An action plan lays out all your tasks to accomplish your goals.

Breaking Down Goals Into Manageable Tasks

Breaking down goals into manageable tasks is a strong strategy that makes your goals less overwhelming and easily achievable. Here are some tips to help you break down your goals:

- **Identify Your Long-Term and Mid-Term Goals:** What do you dream to achieve in the next few years? These long-term goals will take time to achieve, like graduating from university, buying a home, or starting a new business. These goals define who you want to be in the future. Set a time frame for achieving these goals. Next are your mid-term goals, which serve as steppingstones toward your long-term goals. For example, if your long-term goal is to start a business, your mid-term goal can be saving 30% of the capital needed.
- **Focus on Your Short-Term Goals:** Your short-term goals are goals you can achieve readily. They're the actionable tasks that you can start doing now. For example, if your long-term goal is buying a house, your short-term goal can

be researching how much homes cost in the area you want to live in, cutting down expenses, and finding ways of generating passive income. Your short-term goals should be definite and support your long-term goals.

- **Make Your Goals SMART:** Ensure your goals follow the SMART goal-setting strategy. Write them down on paper and keep them where you'll quickly see them daily. Break your goals into action steps to accomplish them within a specified period. Making your goal and action plan difficult is like setting yourself up for frustration.

- **Create Sub-Goals:** First, break down your goals into milestones that will be the major steps toward reaching your goal. Further, break down these milestones into objectives that can be achieved within a short period, like days or weeks.

- **List the Tasks:** Under each sub-goal, list the tasks you must complete. For instance, if your sub-goal is to design a website layout, your tasks include sketching the layout on paper, selecting the color scheme and font, and creating the homepage design.

- **Prioritize and Plan:** Prioritize your tasks based on their significance and impact on achieving the sub-goal. Create a deadline for what needs to be done at a certain time. Using our website example above, you can plan your tasks as follows: Day 1-3: Sketching the layout and choosing the color scheme and font. Day 4-7: Creating the home page design. Day 8-11: Designing the product pages. Day 11-14: Designing the checkout process. This way, you can focus on one task at a time.

- **Track Your Progress:** Set a progress tracker and regularly review it. Celebrate small wins along the way to stay motivated. For example, if your goal is launching an online store, treat yourself to a nice meal after setting up the website.

Prioritizing Tasks and Setting Deadlines

If you have a lot of work on your table, work prioritization allows you to pick out the most important tasks that need to be done first and helps you stay flexible even when new tasks enter. Here are some tips to help you with prioritizing tasks and setting deadlines:

1. Create a Task List: Write down all the assignments you must complete. Listing and keeping them in one place will be a visual reminder of what you must do. Organize your task list into different categories:

- **Daily List:** Short-term goals and high-priority tasks that must be done by the end of the day.
- **Weekly/Monthly List:** Goals for midsize projects that keep you on track.
- **Long-Term List:** Big picture goals you want to achieve over a longer period.

2. Determine Task Deadlines: Next, determine each task's deadlines. Sometimes, this will be straightforward because your boss or client sets the due date. You'll need to estimate how long each step will take for other tasks. Ask yourself: "Can I complete this in a day, or will it take more time?" Review your tasks critically to set accurate timelines. Assign deadlines and focus on those with the nearest due dates first. These should be your top priorities.

3. Assess the Importance of Tasks: As you assign deadlines, also assess the importance of each task. You need to understand your professional goals and company culture to do this well. Consider talking to your boss, coworkers, or clients to see what they think is most important. Understanding their perspectives will help you prioritize effectively.

4. Complete Tasks and Re-Examine Your List: Recheck your list as you finish. Life, especially work, can be unpredictable. New tasks can pop up, and priorities can shift. Be ready to adapt your deadlines and stay flexible.

Strategies for Overcoming Obstacles and Staying on Track

Let's be honest; setting goals is one thing, but sticking to them is a different ball game. Life throws us curveballs, and sometimes, it feels like obstacles are everywhere. But don't worry. Here are some simple strategies to help you overcome those hurdles and stay on track:

1. Identify and Understand Your Obstacles: The first step to overcoming obstacles is discovering what they are. Take a moment to identify what's holding you back. Is it a lack of time, resources, or motivation? Understanding the nature of the obstacle can help you tackle it more effectively.

2. Break Down Big Problems: Sometimes obstacles seem impossible because they're too big to tackle. Break them down into smaller, manageable parts. For instance, if you're working on a big project, break it down into smaller tasks and focus on completing one task at a time. This makes the project feel less overwhelming and more achievable.

3. Stay Flexible: Flexibility is a secret ingredient to overcoming obstacles. Be ready to adjust your plans if something isn't working. Sometimes, the path to your goal might need to change, and that's okay. For example, imagine you're training for a marathon, but you injure your foot. Instead of giving up, you might shift your focus to upper-body workouts until you heal. The goal remains, but the path adjusts.

4. Use Positive Thinking and Visualization: Keeping a positive mindset can help you stay motivated. Visualize your success and remind yourself why you set the goal in the first place. Positive thinking can keep you focused and driven. Picture yourself crossing the finish line of that marathon, feeling proud and accomplished. This mental image can help you push through tough training days.

5. Learn From Your Setbacks: Setbacks are a natural part of any journey. Instead of seeing them as failures, view them as learning opportunities. Each setback teaches you something new about yourself and your approach. For instance, if you fail a test, instead of getting discouraged, analyze what went wrong. Did you need more study time? Was the study method ineffective? Use this information to improve your strategy for next time.

OVERCOMING OBSTACLES AND EXCUSES

Life isn't always a smooth ride, and sometimes it feels like the universe is playing a game of "Let's see how many obstacles we can throw at you today." These hurdles can slow us down, whether it's procrastination, self-doubt, or just plain bad luck. But don't worry! We will tackle these challenges with a positive attitude and unmatched resilience. Buckle up because we're about to turn those obstacles into stepping stones and those excuses into motivation!

Identifying Common Barriers to Goal Achievement

Recognizing the barriers below allows for the development of strategies to overcome them, leading to more effective goal achievement.

1. Lack of Clarity and Focus: One of the biggest hurdles to goal achievement is needing a specific goal. If your goal is too vague, like "I want to be successful," it's hard to know where to start. Instead, make your goals SMART. For example, setting your goal as "I want to become a project manager within two years by completing a certification and leading two major projects" gives you a clear target to aim for.

2. Procrastination: Procrastination is the enemy of progress. It's easy to think, "I'll do it tomorrow," but tomorrow turns into next week and month. To beat procrastination, break your goal into smaller tasks. Start with something simple to build momentum. For instance, if you need to write a report, draft an outline today.

3. Fear of Failure: Fear can be a huge roadblock. You might fear failing and looking foolish, which can prevent you from trying. Change your perspective by viewing failures as lessons. Remember, every successful person has faced failures. Think of Thomas Edison, who famously said he didn't fail 1,000 times but found 1,000 ways that didn't work when inventing the light bulb.

4. Lack of Resources: Insufficient resources, such as time, money, or knowledge, can stall your progress. Identify what you're missing and find ways to get it. For instance, if you lack skills, consider online courses or workshops. If time is an issue, prioritize your tasks and delegate where possible

5. Poor Time Management: Poor time management can make your goals seem unachievable. Create a daily or weekly schedule with specific time slots for working on your goals. Planners, calendars, or apps can keep you organized. For instance, block out an hour each morning for focused work on your main project before checking emails or attending meetings.

6. Negative Mindset: Your mindset is crucial in helping you achieve your goals. If you constantly think, "I can't do this," you're setting yourself up for failure. Practice positive thinking and surround yourself with supportive people. Replace negative thoughts with affirmations like, "I can handle this" or "I'm making progress every day."

7. Distractions: Distractions are everywhere, whether it's social media, TV, or even household chores. Set up a dedicated work-space and minimize distractions by turning off notifications and setting specific break times. For instance, use the Pomodoro Technique: work for 25 minutes, then take a 5-minute break. This can help maintain focus and productivity.

Strategies for Overcoming Procrastination and Self-Doubt

Procrastination and self-doubt are like those annoying, uninvited guests who show up and spoil the fun of achieving our goals. But don't worry; there are effective strategies to kick them out of your life. Let's explore some practical tips.

1. Break Your Tasks Into Smaller Steps: One of the best ways to tackle procrastination is to chunk big tasks into smaller, manageable pieces. This strategy makes daunting tasks feel more manageable. For example, if you need to write a report, start with smaller steps like researching, outlining, and drafting one section at a time. This approach not only reduces procrastination but also increases productivity and motivation

2. Use Positive Self-Talk: Self-doubt often creeps in with negative self-talk like, "I can't do this" or "I'm not good enough." Fight these thoughts and replace them with positive affirmations. Tell yourself, "I can handle this" or "I can achieve my goals." This shift in mindset can boost your confidence and reduce feelings of inadequacy.

3. Create a Conducive Work Environment: Your environment dramatically influences productivity. Create a dedicated workspace free from distractions, keep it organized, and equip it with everything you need. If social media or other distractions are problematic, use apps that block them during work hours.

4. Practice Mindfulness and Stress Management: Sometimes procrastination and self-doubt stem from stress and anxiety. Mindfulness practices, such as meditation or deep-breathing exercises, can help calm your mind and improve focus. Regular exercise and healthy sleep patterns contribute to better mental health and productivity.

Cultivating Resilience in the Face of Setbacks

Building resilience isn't about avoiding problems; instead, it's about developing the ability to adapt and recover from challenges. Here are some ways to cultivate resilience:

First, it's crucial to maintain a positive outlook. When setbacks occur, it's easy to get bogged down by negative thoughts. Instead, try to reframe the situation. Ask yourself what you can learn from the experience and how it can strengthen you. This mindset shift can turn obstacles into opportunities for growth.

Also, having friends, family, or colleagues to talk to can provide emotional support and practical advice when facing difficulties. Sharing your experiences with others can help you see things from different perspectives and find new solutions.

Practicing self-care is also vital for resilience. Taking care of your physical and mental health can improve your overall well-being and make you more equipped to handle stress. Regular exercise, a healthy diet, and sufficient sleep are essential. Additionally, activities like meditation or hobbies that you enjoy can help reduce stress and recharge your energy.

Lastly, developing problem-solving skills can enhance your resilience. When confronted with a setback, take a step back and assess the situation. Identify the problem, brainstorm possible solutions, and evaluate their pros and cons. This approach can help you navigate challenges effectively and find the best action.

Accountability and Tracking Progress

Achieving your goals isn't just about setting them; it's also about staying on track and holding yourself accountable. The sections that follow will dive into how accountability partners and support systems, using technology and tools, and celebrating milestones can help you maintain momentum and stay motivated.

The Role of Accountability Partners and Support Systems

Accountability partners and support systems can make a significant difference in achieving goals. These elements provide encouragement, motivation, and the nudge to stay on track and move forward.

An accountability partner helps you focus on your goals by regularly checking your progress. This could be a friend, family member, or colleague who understands your objectives and is committed to helping you succeed. When someone else is aware of your goals and monitors your progress, it becomes harder to slack off. These regular check-ins foster a sense of responsibility and significantly boost your chances of success.

Support systems also play a crucial role. These include mentors, peer groups, or online communities that offer advice, share experiences, and provide motivation. Engaging with a group of people who have similar goals can be incredibly inspiring. You share perspectives, suggest new strategies, and celebrate each other's success. This collective energy keeps you motivated and focused on your path.

According to FasterCapital, accountability partners and support systems provide a structured environment where you can openly discuss challenges and celebrate achievements (Finding Inspiration in Role Models and Success Stories, 2024). This structure helps maintain motivation and tackle obstacles head-on. These relationships' emotional and practical support can help you push through difficult times and stay committed to your goals.

Moreover, research supports the effectiveness of accountability. A study by the American Society of Training and Development (A.S.T.D.) found that if you commit to someone, you have a 65% chance of completing a goal. If you have a specific accountability appointment with that person, you will increase your chance of success by up to 95% (Hanke, 2018).

Having an accountability partner or a support system doesn't just help track progress; it also helps you stay motivated during tough times. When setbacks occur, these partners can offer support and help you get back on track. This shared commitment helps build resilience and keeps you moving forward.

For instance, if you're working toward a fitness goal, having a workout buddy joining you for regular exercise sessions can motivate you. Similarly, if you're working on a professional project, having a colleague to brainstorm with and provide feedback can make a big difference.

Generally, incorporating accountability partners and support systems into your goal-setting process can significantly enhance your chances of success. Whether through regular check-ins or the broader support of a community, having others involved in your journey makes the path to achieving your goals much smoother and more enjoyable. These relationships provide accountability, encouragement, and support, making pursuing your goals a more rewarding experience.

Utilizing Technology and Tools to Track Progress

Keeping track of your goals can sometimes feel like a daunting task. Luckily, technology offers a range of tools to make this process much smoother and more efficient.

Why Use Technology?

Using tech tools to track your goals has many benefits. They can help you stay organized, remind you of deadlines, and visually represent your progress, which can be incredibly motivating. What's more? Most of these tools are designed to be user-friendly, making it easy to get started.

Popular Tools for Tracking Goals

1. **Project Management Apps:** Tools like Trello and Asana are excellent for breaking big projects into manageable tasks. You can create boards, lists, and cards to organize work, set deadlines, and track progress. These tools also allow for collaboration, making them perfect for working with a team.
2. **Habit Trackers:** Apps like Habitica and Streaks help you build and maintain new habits. By marking off each day you complete a task, these apps create a visual streak that encourages you to keep going. It's a simple but effective way to stay accountable.
3. **Goal-Setting Platforms:** GoalsOnTrack and Tability provide structured goal-setting frameworks. They help you set SMART goals and track your progress with detailed analytics and progress reports. These platforms often include features like progress bars and milestone markers, which can be incredibly satisfying to update.

Some advantages of using technology for tracking your progress include:

Integration With Daily Life: Many of these tools integrate seamlessly with other applications you use daily. For example, Trello and Asana can sync with your calendar and email, sending reminders and updates directly to your inbox. This integration ensures that your goal-tracking efforts are always at the forefront without needing to manage multiple systems separately.

Benefit From Visual Tracking: Visual aids like charts and graphs can provide a clear picture of your progress. Seeing your tasks checked off and your goals getting closer can be a powerful motivator. Many apps include dashboards that offer an at-a-glance view of your current status, making staying motivated and focused on your end goals easier.

Leveraging technology to track your progress keeps you organized and provides continuous motivation. Using the right tools, you can break down your goals into manageable tasks, visually track your progress, and integrate goal setting into your daily routine. So, find the best tools for you and start tracking your way to success!

Celebrating Milestones and Staying Motivated

Achieving goals is like running a marathon. It's not just about reaching the finish line; it's also about celebrating the progress you make along the way. Recognizing and celebrating milestones is critical to staying motivated and maintaining momentum.

Why Celebrate Milestones?

Celebrating milestones isn't just about giving yourself a pat on the back; it has real psychological benefits. Recognizing your progress can boost your motivation, increase your confidence, and make the journey toward your goal more enjoyable. When you celebrate, you acknowledge your hard work and progress, reinforcing positive behavior and encouraging you to keep pushing forward.

How to Celebrate Milestones

Celebrating milestones can be done in various ways, depending on personal preferences and the significance of the achievement. Here are some ideas:

1. Personal Rewards: Treat yourself to something you enjoy. This could be as simple as a nice meal, a day off, or buying something you've wanted. The key is to choose something that feels like a reward to you.

2. Share With Others: Sharing your achievements with friends, family, or colleagues can enhance your accomplishment. It also provides you with a support system that can cheer you on and celebrate your successes with you.

3. Reflect on Your Progress: Take a moment to reflect on how far you've come. Write down what you've achieved, how you did it, and what you've learned. This reflection can provide valuable insights and reinforce your motivation to keep going.

4. Visual Reminders: Use visual aids like charts or checklists to mark your progress. Seeing a visual representation of your progress can be incredibly satisfying and motivating. For instance, crossing off completed tasks on a checklist can give you a sense of achievement.

To keep pushing, you also need to stay motivated. This is more than just celebrating milestones. It's about keeping your end goal in sight and continuously reminding yourself why you started in the first place. Setting clear, specific goals is crucial as it provides a target to aim for and helps maintain focus.

Maintaining a positive attitude is also key, especially when things get tough. Surrounding yourself with positive influences and regularly reminding yourself of your successes can boost your spirits and keep you moving forward. It's important to focus on what you've achieved so far and use that as motivation to keep going.

Regular check-ins are another essential component of staying motivated. Periodically reviewing your goals and progress helps ensure that you remain on track and allows you to make any necessary adjustments. By consistently monitoring your progress, you can stay aligned with your objectives and maintain the momentum needed to achieve your goals.

KEY TAKEAWAYS

- Setting clear and specific goals helps provide direction and focus, making it easier to stay on track.
- The SMART (Specific, Measurable, Achievable, Relevant,

and Time-Bound) framework ensures your objectives are realistic and attainable.

- Tracking progress and celebrating small wins keeps you motivated and aware of how far you've come.
- Recognizing these milestones helps maintain enthusiasm and commitment to your long-term goals.
- Utilizing support systems and technology can significantly enhance your ability to stay committed. Accountability partners and progress-tracking tools offer additional support and motivation.
- Breaking down large goals into manageable tasks, prioritizing them, and setting deadlines are crucial steps in creating an effective action plan. This makes achieving even the most ambitious goals feel more attainable and manageable.

In the next chapter, we'll discuss how to master time management, how to adopt the proper techniques for prioritization and decision-making, as well as some hacks to make you become a time management guru.

CHAPTER 3
MASTERING TIME
MANAGEMENT

*Time is the scarcest resource, and unless it is managed, nothing else can
be managed.*

PETER DRUCKER

Time is something we all wish we had more of, yet it's often the
one resource that seems to slip through our fingers the quickest. In
this chapter, we're diving into time management to equip you with
a skill that can transform your work and life.

We'll start with learning to prioritize tasks and activities, using
tools like the Eisenhower Matrix to separate the urgent from the
important. This will help you make better decisions about where to
focus your energy. Next, we'll explore creating a daily routine that
boosts productivity and balances work, leisure, and self-care.
You'll learn why a structured schedule can make your day
smoother and more manageable.

Finally, we'll introduce you to the Pomodoro Technique and other
productivity hacks. These methods harness the power of focused
work and regular breaks, ensuring you stay fresh and efficient

throughout the day. So, let's get started on this journey to take control of your time and make every minute count!

PRIORITIZING TASKS AND ACTIVITIES

You might start your day at work to be very productive. Yet, as the day rolls on, you'll find yourself in an ocean of multiple urgent tasks and an unending task list. The goals you initially set out to accomplish that day get pushed to one side. Well, you aren't alone in this. Without a well-planned process for prioritizing tasks at work, it will feel like you're playing catch-up. This section will discuss techniques for prioritization and decision-making and how to eliminate time-wasting activities and distractions.

The Eisenhower Matrix: Urgent vs. Important

Do you ever feel like your to-do list is a mile long, and you need help figuring out where to start? That's where the Eisenhower Matrix comes in. Named after Dwight D. Eisenhower, the 34th President of the United States, this tool helps you sort tasks by urgency and importance, making it easier to focus on the right things at the right time.

The Eisenhower Matrix is a simple productivity and time management framework that helps you prioritize your tasks according to importance and urgency.

Also called the Eisenhower Box or Eisenhower Decision Matrix, this framework consists of a drawing of a four-boxed square with an X-axis labeled urgent and not urgent and a Y-axis labeled important and not important. Here's a breakdown of what's included in the four quadrants:

1. **Urgent and Important:** These tasks need immediate attention and usually have consequences if completed later. Think of deadlines, emergencies, and crises. For instance, if you have a project due tomorrow, it goes here.

2. **Important but Not Urgent:** These tasks contribute to your long-term goals but don't need immediate attention. Planning, exercising, and learning new skills fall into this category. They might not be screaming for your attention now, but they're crucial for personal and professional growth.

3. **Urgent but Not Important:** These tasks demand immediate action but don't necessarily contribute to your long-term goals. Often, they're interruptions or distractions like answering non-urgent emails or attending certain meetings. Whenever possible, try to delegate these tasks.

4. **Not Urgent and Not Important:** These are the tasks that could be more time-sensitive and valuable to your goals. Activities like scrolling through social media or binge-watching TV shows typically fall into this category. Reducing or eliminating these can free up time for more important activities.

Implementing the Eisenhower's Matrix: Project Manager's Daily Tasks

Let's break down a typical workday scenario using the Eisenhower Matrix to illustrate how to prioritize tasks effectively.

Urgent and Important

Client Presentation Due Tomorrow: You have a major presentation due for a client meeting tomorrow. This requires immediate attention, as missing this deadline could seriously affect your relationship with the client and your brand's reputation.

Important but Not Urgent

Strategic Planning for Next Quarter: You need to plan your team's goals and strategies for the next quarter. While this isn't due immediately, it's crucial for your long-term success and ensuring your team is well-prepared for future projects.

Urgent but Not Important

Daily Status Update Emails: You receive numerous emails daily that require quick responses but aren't crucial to your long-term goals. Responding to these emails is necessary to maintain smooth daily operations but doesn't significantly impact your overall objectives.

Not Urgent and Not Important

Social Media Browsing: You occasionally check social media during work hours. This activity doesn't contribute to your goals and can be a major time-wasting.

Applying the Matrix

- **Focus on Urgent and Important:** Start working on the client presentation to ensure it's ready for tomorrow.
- **Schedule Time for Important but Not Urgent:** Allocate specific times in your calendar for strategic planning and your online course. These tasks are crucial for long-term success and should be addressed.
- **Delegate Urgent but Not Important:** Delegate a team member to check emails or set specific times to quickly address status update emails without letting them interrupt more critical work.
- **Minimize or Eliminate Urgent and Unimportant Tasks:** Limit social media use by setting strict boundaries (e.g., only checking during lunch breaks) and staying focused on more impactful tasks.

Using the Eisenhower Matrix helps you prioritize tasks effectively. Instead of just working through your to-do list in a linear fashion, you can strategically decide what to tackle first. So, next time you're overwhelmed, take a step back, draw your matrix, and start categorizing your tasks. You need clarity to get back on track and stay productive.

Techniques for Effective Prioritization and Decision-Making

Getting your priorities straight and making smart decisions is like juggling multiple balls simultaneously. But with the proper techniques, you can turn this into a smooth, organized process. Let's dive into some effective ways to prioritize and make decisions.

1. The MoSCoW Method

The MoSCoW Method helps you categorize tasks based on their importance and urgency. It has four categories which are:

- **Must-Have:** Essential tasks that need to be done immediately.
- **Should-Have:** Important tasks that aren't critical.
- **Could-Have:** Nice-to-have tasks that aren't crucial.
- **Won't-Have:** Tasks that can be postponed or skipped.

For example, if you're working on a project, the must-have tasks might be meeting key deadlines, the should-have tasks could involve adding extra features, the could-have tasks might include minor improvements, and the won't-have tasks are those that can wait. However, if you've got a lot of work that needs delegation, there might be better methods for you.

2. The Pareto Principle (80/20 rule)

The Pareto Principle suggests that 80% of results come from 20% of efforts. Focus on the 20% of tasks that will produce most of your results. This means you should identify the most important tasks that offer the most value, prioritize them, and allocate more resources accordingly. If you're a student, this might mean studying the most critical topics and covering most of your exams.

3. The Eisenhower Matrix

We've already covered this, but to recap briefly: Sort your tasks into four categories: urgent and important, important but not urgent, urgent but not important, and neither urgent nor important. This helps you prioritize what needs immediate attention and what can be scheduled for later.

4. The A.B.C.D.E. Method

Developed by Brian Tracy, the A.B.C.D.E. method assigns a letter to each task on your list:

- **A** tasks are very important and must be done.
- **B** tasks are important but less crucial than A tasks.
- **C** tasks are nice to do but optional.
- **D** tasks can be delegated to someone else.
- **E** tasks can be eliminated.

This helps you quickly see which tasks need your immediate attention and which ones can be handled by others.

5. Decision Matrix

A Decision Matrix helps you evaluate and prioritize a list of options. You list your options as rows and criteria as columns. Then, you score each option based on each criterion, helping you make a well-informed decision. This is great for making complex decisions where you need to consider multiple factors.

Eliminating Time-Wasting Activities and Distractions

Time-wasting activities and distractions can seriously impede productivity, making staying on track with your goals challenging. But how can you eliminate them? This section covers that!

1. **Identify Your Time Wasters:** The first step to eliminating time-wasting activities is identifying what they are.

Common culprits include excessive social media use, unnecessary meetings, and constant email checking. Having frequent notifications can fragment your focus and waste significant time throughout the day. Keeping a time log for a few days can help you see where your time goes and spot patterns.

2. **Cut Down on Notifications:** One effective strategy to eliminate distractions is to reduce notifications. Consider turning off non-essential notifications on your phone and computer. This reduces the urge to check your devices constantly. You can also schedule specific times to check emails and messages instead of responding to every message immediately.

3. **Create a Focused Work Environment:** One of the best ways to improve productivity is by creating a workspace that minimizes distractions. Consider setting up a dedicated work area away from high-traffic zones and noise. Use tools like noise-canceling headphones or white noise machines to help maintain focus.

4. **Prioritize Important Tasks:** Priority! Priority! And priority! By using techniques like the Eisenhower Matrix, which we discussed earlier, prioritize tasks based on their urgency and importance. This helps you focus on high-priority activities that contribute directly to your goals while delegating or postponing less critical tasks.

5. **Limit Multitasking:** You must be shocked to see this! Isn't it some form of discipline to be able to multitask? Well, multitasking also has its downside, which is that it can decrease your productivity. Focusing on one task at a time can improve your efficiency and the quality of your work.

6. **Use Technology Wisely:** While technology can be a source of distraction, it can also be a powerful tool for managing your time effectively. Use productivity apps and tools to schedule tasks, set reminders, and track progress. Tools

like Trello, Asana, or even simple to-do list apps can keep you organized and focused.

CREATING A DAILY ROUTINE

Establishing a daily routine is a powerful way to bring structure and efficiency into your life. It's about designing your day to optimize productivity while balancing work, leisure, and self-care. Let's take a more detailed look at creating routine and balancing work and self-care:

The Benefits of a Structured Daily Schedule

Here are some key benefits of having a well-structured daily schedule:

1. Boosts Productivity

A well-planned routine helps you prioritize your tasks, ensuring that you focus on the most important ones first. By setting aside specific times for your work, leisure, and personal projects, you're more likely to stay on track and avoid the pitfalls of procrastination. It serves as a roadmap for your day, guiding you from task to task efficiently.

2. Reduces Stress

Knowing what to expect each day can significantly reduce stress and anxiety. When you have a clear plan, there's less room for uncertainty and last-minute scrambles. This predictability allows you to manage your time better and reduces the stress of handling tasks at the last minute.

3. Improves Health and Well-Being

A daily routine can positively impact your physical and mental health. Regular meals, exercise, and sleep schedules help maintain a healthy lifestyle. Additionally, setting times for relaxation and hobbies can enhance your emotional well-being, giving you a much-needed break from work and daily pressures.

4. Enhances Self-Discipline

Sticking to a routine builds self-discipline and helps form good habits. Over time, these habits become second nature, making staying committed to your goals and responsibilities easier. This consistency can lead to long-term success in various areas, from career to personal growth.

5. Frees Up Mental Space

When your day is planned out, you don't have to waste mental energy deciding what to do next. This mental clarity can lead to more creativity and better problem-solving abilities. With a routine, you can focus more on the quality of your work rather than constantly juggling tasks and decisions.

Balancing Work, Leisure, and Self-Care

Finding the right balance between work, leisure, and self-care is essential for a fulfilling and healthy life. This can be hard, especially when work demands pile up and personal responsibilities feel endless. However, striking this balance is crucial for your overall well-being and productivity. Let's explore how you can achieve it:

1. **Understand the Importance of Balance:** First, recognize that balance is key to avoiding burnout and maintaining happiness. When you work too much without taking time for yourself, stress levels rise, and your productivity level decreases. On the flip side, too much leisure without focus can leave you feeling unfulfilled. The goal is to find a sweet spot where all aspects of your life are nurtured.
2. **Set Boundaries:** Setting clear boundaries is one of the most effective ways to balance work and personal life. This means defining your work hours and sticking to them.

Turn off work notifications after those hours and create a dedicated workspace. This separation helps you fully engage in leisure activities and self-care without intruding on work stress.

3. **Prioritize Self-Care:** Self-care isn't just about pampering yourself; it's about taking proactive steps to maintain physical and mental health. Schedule a regular time for activities that make you happy and relax your mind, whether it's a daily walk, reading a book, or practicing mindfulness. Remember, taking care of yourself enhances your ability to handle work and personal responsibilities more effectively.

4. **Integrate Leisure Into Your Routine:** Leisure time is essential for relaxation and mental rejuvenation. Plan activities that you enjoy and make them a regular part of your routine. This could be anything from hobbies and sports to spending time with loved ones. Engaging in leisure activities can boost your mood and creativity, making you more productive when you return to work.

5. **Flexibility Is the Key:** Life is unpredictable, and work or personal demands sometimes require more time. Be flexible and adjust your schedule as needed without feeling guilty. The aim is to balance over the long term, not to be perfect every day, and to burn out after some days. Be easy on yourself and adapt as circumstances change.

THE POMODORO TECHNIQUE AND OTHER PRODUCTIVITY HACKS

Have you ever wished you could unlock the secret to staying focused and productive, even when distractions lurk around every corner? Well, I've got the key, and all you need to do to get it is to keep reading! In this section, we'll explore some strategies that can turn your productivity up a notch. Let's discover how these methods can transform your approach to self-discipline from the famous Pomodoro Technique to other clever productivity hacks.

Harnessing the Power of Focused Bursts of Work

Have you ever noticed how sometimes your best work happens when you're in the zone, fully immersed in what you're doing? Turns out, there's a name for that magical state: *flow*. It's when your productivity skyrockets because you're super focused, and everything clicks. One way to tap into this flow is through short bursts of concentrated effort. Imagine tackling a task with all your energy for, say, 25 minutes straight. This technique, known as the Pomodoro Technique, helps you stay on track and prevents burnout by giving you built-in breaks.

Understanding the Pomodoro Technique

The Pomodoro Technique is a time management method designed to enhance productivity by breaking work into intervals, traditionally 25 minutes in length, separated by short 5-minute breaks. Francesco Cirillo developed the technique in the late 1980s, inspired by a tomato-shaped kitchen timer (Fun fact: "Pomodoro" means tomato in Italian).

The Pomodoro Technique helps eliminate distractions and promotes deep concentration on the task by working in short, focused bursts. Breaking tasks into manageable intervals makes daunting projects more achievable, increasing productivity and a sense of accomplishment. Also, regular breaks between Pomodoros prevent mental fatigue and burnout, allowing you to sustain high productivity levels throughout the day.

Picture this, you're writing a book. Using the Pomodoro Technique, you dedicate one Pomodoro to outlining a chapter, another to drafting the introduction, and so on. This structured approach ensures steady progress while maintaining focus and clarity.

How It Works

- **Set a Timer:** Choose a task and set a timer for 25 minutes (one Pomodoro).
- **Work Intensely:** Focus on the task until the timer rings, avoiding distractions and interruptions.
- **Take a Break:** When the Pomodoro ends, take a short break (typically 5 minutes) to recharge.
- **Repeat the Same Process:** After completing four Pomodoros, take a more extended break (around 15-30 minutes) to rest and rejuvenate.

Tips for Success With the Pomodoro Technique

By following the tips below, you can maximize the effectiveness of the Pomodoro Technique and enhance your productivity.

- **Choose Appropriate Tasks:** Not all tasks are equally suited to the Pomodoro Technique. To get the most out of it, prioritize tasks that require focused attention and can be broken down into smaller, actionable steps. Examples include writing, studying, coding, or any task that demands concentration without constant interruptions.
- **Plan Pomodoro Sessions Strategically:** Before starting a Pomodoro session, take a moment to plan what you aim to accomplish during that interval. Setting clear objectives helps maintain focus and ensures you make progress toward your larger goals. Use the initial minutes of each Pomodoro to outline tasks or review notes, then dive into the main work once you're fully engaged.
- **Use Tools and Apps:** Several digital and smartphone apps are designed specifically for the Pomodoro Technique. These tools help you track your Pomodoro sessions, alert you when to take breaks, and provide statistics on your productivity over time. Popular apps include Forest, Focus

Booster, and Pomodone. Experiment with different tools to find one that aligns with your preferences and workflow.

- **Customize Pomodoro Lengths:** While the traditional Pomodoro length is 25 minutes of work followed by a 5-minute break, it's essential to customize these intervals based on your personal preferences and the nature of your tasks. Some people find that shorter Pomodoros (e.g., 15 minutes of work) are more effective for tasks requiring intense concentration, while others may prefer longer intervals for tasks that require deeper immersion. Experiment with different lengths to determine what works best for you.

Incorporating Breaks and Restorative Activities Into Your Day

Do you ever feel like you're constantly pushing through tasks without a moment to catch your breath? Taking breaks isn't just a luxury—it's essential for maintaining productivity, creativity, and overall well-being. Regular breaks are crucial for maintaining mental clarity, focus, and productivity. The brain can only sustain high levels of concentration for a limited time before needing a rest. By stepping away from work periodically, whether for a few minutes or longer, we allow our minds to recharge and return to tasks with renewed energy and efficiency.

Contrary to the belief that constant work leads to greater productivity, breaks enhance our ability to perform well. Breaks prevent burnout, reduce stress levels, and improve our mood, contributing to better decision-making and problem-solving skills. Resting and recharging make us more likely to approach tasks with a fresh perspective and creativity.

Restorative Activities to Engage in During Your Break Time

Restorative activities can help you recharge and return to work with renewed energy and focus. Below are some activities you can engage in during your break time:

1. **Physical Activity:** Physical activities such as taking a short walk, stretching, or practicing yoga can alleviate physical tension and stimulate circulation. For example, a brief stroll around the office or home can loosen stiff muscles and increase blood flow to the brain, improving mental clarity and focus.

2. **Mindfulness and Relaxation:** Activities like deep breathing exercises, meditation, or simply a few minutes to close your eyes and clear your mind can significantly reduce stress levels and enhance overall well-being. For instance, practicing deep breathing techniques for a few minutes can lower heart rate and calm the mind, promoting relaxation and mental rejuvenation.

3. **Social Interaction:** Connecting with colleagues, friends, or family members during breaks can provide emotional support, improve mood, and prevent feelings of isolation. Whether sharing a laugh with coworkers over a coffee break or chatting with a friend on the phone, social interactions during breaks contribute to a positive work environment and emotional well-being.

Experimenting With Different Productivity Methods to Find What Works Best for You

There are many productivity methods out there, and what works for one might not work for another. Finding your best productivity method involves experimenting with different approaches until you discover the perfect fit.

If you struggle with procrastination you can experiment with the Pomodoro Technique to break tasks into manageable chunks and stay focused. Alternatively, if you thrive on structure, time blocking could be your game-changer, allowing you to allocate specific hours for different projects and minimize distractions.

Let's explore how you can maneuver your productivity strategies to suit your unique style.

- **Time Blocking:** Allocate specific time blocks for different tasks or types of work throughout your day. It helps create structure and prevents multitasking.
- **Getting Things Done (GTD):** Organize tasks into actionable items, projects, and priorities. This approach focuses on clearing mental clutter and boosting productivity.
- **Eat That Frog:** Tackle your most challenging or essential task in the morning. This method promotes a sense of accomplishment and sets a productive tone for the day.
- **Bullet Journaling:** This method combines scheduling, task management, and note-taking in a customizable journal format. It provides flexibility and encourages creativity in planning.
- **Be Flexible:** Always be ready to change your productivity method if it isn't working. Remember that what works for one might not work for the other.

KEY TAKEAWAYS

- Use the Eisenhower Matrix to categorize tasks by urgency and importance. This helps you focus on what matters most and manage your time effectively.
- Daily routines boost productivity by prioritizing tasks, reducing stress, and enhancing overall well-being.
- Adopt the Pomodoro Technique to enhance focus and productivity. You can maintain high concentration levels and avoid burnout by breaking work into focused intervals followed by short breaks.
- Identify and eliminate time-wasting activities and distractions, such as excessive social media use and

unnecessary meetings. This will help you stay on track with your goals and maintain productivity.

In the next chapter, we'll learn how to develop the muscle of self-control through healthy habits and effectively manage stress and negative emotions.

CHAPTER 4
CULTIVATING SELF-CONTROL

The more you can say no to distractions, the more you can say yes to your dreams.

UNKNOWN

You can have the power to stay focused on your goals, no matter what temptations come your way—that's what self-control does. Let's unlock the secrets to cultivating self-control, a crucial skill that can transform your life. Think of self-control as a muscle; the more you exercise it, the stronger it becomes.

This chapter will explore the psychology of instant gratification and learn why resisting temptations can be so challenging. We'll also discuss how understanding your triggers and mastering emotional regulation allows you to navigate life's hurdles more easily and resiliently.

We'll take a look at the science of habit formation and how building healthy habits can support your journey toward self-discipline. Whether you aim to break bad habits or establish new, positive ones, this chapter provides the tools you need to stay consistent and overcome obstacles.

Let's enhance your self-control so you can say "yes" to your dreams more often and build the disciplined life you aspire to lead.

UNDERSTANDING TEMPTATION AND IMPULSE

Have you ever wondered why it's so difficult to resist that second slice of cake or to stay focused on work when social media is just a click away? The answer lies in our brain's natural inclination toward instant gratification. Temptation can be defined as the desire to do something that you rationally know might not be in your best interest to do. But why is it so hard to resist? Keep reading to find out!

The Psychology of Instant Gratification

The psychology of instant gratification explains why we often choose immediate pleasure over long-term benefits. This behavior is deeply rooted in the way our brains are wired. When we choose immediate rewards, our brain's system kicks into high gear, releasing dopamine, a neurotransmitter. This immediate rush of pleasure reinforces the behavior, making us more likely to seek similar quick fixes in the future (Bastos, 2024).

Evolutionary psychology explains why we're often more driven to choose instant pleasure than long-term rewards. Our ancestors lived in a time of uncertainty, where the future was very unpredictable, making delayed gratification a risky option as they couldn't be sure of what the future held. Choosing immediate pleasure helped them meet their needs, like food and shelter. This has shaped our decision-making process to forego a future reward and give in to instant benefits.

A real-life example of instant gratification is online shopping. With a few clicks, you can buy almost anything and have it delivered quickly. This convenience feeds our desire for immediate gratification, often leading to impulsive purchases. The ease of online shopping can increase impulsive buying behaviors, as the instant pleasure of a new purchase outweighs the potential long-term financial consequences. This constant availability of instant gratification can lead to addictive behaviors. Studies indicate that frequent use of social media activates the brain's reward system in much the same way as other addictive behaviors, making it hard to break the habit (Białaszek et al., 2015).

While it feels good at the moment, relying too much on instant gratification can have significant downsides. It can interfere with our ability to achieve long-term goals and maintain healthy habits. For instance, preferring fast food over cooking at home might save time and satisfy immediate hunger, but it can lead to health issues in the long term.

Instant gratification also hurts our productivity. You could be working on an important project, but you keep getting distracted by notifications on your phone. Each time you check your phone, you get a small reward—a new message, a like, or an interesting post. These distractions can add up, making it difficult to focus on the task and delaying your progress toward completing your project.

The first step to managing instant gratification is understanding the psychology behind it. Knowing that our brains are wired to seek quick rewards allows us to be more mindful of our choices. For example, recognizing that you might be reaching for your phone out of habit rather than necessity can help you consciously decide to put it away and focus on your work.

Another helpful insight comes from "delay discounting," which tends to devalue rewards that aren't immediately available. This concept explains why it's often more challenging to stick to long-term goals, such as saving money or maintaining a healthy diet. By becoming aware of this tendency, we can work on strategies to counteract it, such as setting smaller, more immediate milestones that lead to a larger goal (Bastos, 2024).

Recognizing Triggers and Cues That Lead to Impulsive Behavior

Recognizing the triggers and cues that lead to impulsive behavior is essential for improving self-control in everyday life. These triggers can be subtle, often slipping under our radar, but they significantly impact our day-to-day lives.

What Are Triggers?

Triggers are specific events, environments, or emotions that push you to act impulsively. They can be external, like certain places or people, or internal, like feelings of stress or boredom. For instance, many people find that stress triggers impulsive eating. You mostly focus on short-term pleasure and don't consider the long-term effects before reaching for comfort foods.

An excellent way to understand your triggers is to keep a journal of your impulsive behaviors. Note each instance's circumstances, including where you were, who you were with, and what you felt. Over time, you'll notice a pattern that can help you identify your triggers.

Common Triggers

Identifying triggers can help in managing and mitigating their impact on well-being and productivity. Common triggers can include:

1. **Emotional States:** Feelings of anxiety, depression, and stress are common triggers for impulsive actions like overeating, shopping sprees, or binge-watching. These emotions can drive you to seek immediate comfort, even if it's not healthy in the long run.
2. **Environmental Cues:** Places and situations often serve as triggers. For example, walking past a bakery might trigger

a decision to buy a pastry, even if you weren't hungry. Similarly, specific social settings, like parties, can trigger excessive drinking and smoking.

3. **Social Influences:** Being around certain people can also trigger impulsive behavior. Peer pressure or wanting to fit in with a group can lead to impulsive decisions, such as spending money you hadn't planned to or engaging in risky activities.

What Are Cues?

Cues are the signals that prompt a habitual response. They're the starting points of a habit loop, which consists of a cue, a routine, and a reward. For instance, if checking your phone is a habitual response to feeling bored, boredom is the cue; checking your phone is routine, and the pleasure from seeing new notifications is the reward (Bastos, 2024).

Common Cues

Common cues that can trigger behaviors or reactions include:

1. **Time of Day:** Certain times of the day can act as cues. For example, you might habitually be snacking in the late afternoon. Recognizing this pattern can help you find healthier ways to manage that period.
2. **Locations:** Being in specific places can be a cue for certain behaviors. Your living room might cue relaxation and binge-watching, while your office might cue working or checking important emails. Identifying these cues can help you create more productive environments.
3. **Preceding Events:** Activities or events that happen right before an impulsive behavior can serve as cues. For example, if you always buy a coffee after your morning workout, the end of the workout acts as a cue for the coffee purchase.

Managing Triggers and Cues

Managing triggers and cues involves several strategies to mitigate their impact on behavior and well-being. By actively managing triggers and cues, individuals can enhance their ability to respond thoughtfully rather than react impulsively, fostering healthier behaviors and emotional well-being. Below are some strategies:

1. **Avoidance:** Try as much as you can to avoid known triggers. If stress leads to impulsive eating, find stress-reducing activities like exercise or meditation to replace the eating habit.
2. **Substitution:** Replace impulsive behaviors with healthier alternatives. If boredom triggers mindless snacking, replace it with a hobby or activity that keeps your hands and mind busy.
3. **Mindfulness:** Practice mindfulness to become more aware of your triggers and cues. This awareness can help you take a pause and choose a more deliberate response rather than acting impulsively.4.
4. **Environment Control:** Modify your environment to become fit for a healthy lifestyle. If you snack impulsively, keep healthy snacks readily available and remove junk food from your sight.

Strategies for Strengthening Self-Control Muscle

Below are some strategies for strengthening your self-control muscle. By consistently practicing these strategies, you can improve decision-making, maintain healthy habits, and achieve long-term success in various aspects of life.

1. **Make Your Goals Simple:** Consider something you want to achieve, like drinking more water or studying regularly. Break it into small steps, like drinking one extra glass daily or studying for 30 minutes.

2. **Practice Good Habits:** Start small with habits you want to stick to, like going for a walk or eating veggies during dinner. Practicing good habits regularly makes it easier to say "no" to things you shouldn't do.

3. **Imagine Success:** Picture yourself acing that test or resisting the urge to buy something you don't need. It's like giving yourself a pep talk in your head.

4. **Be Kind to Yourself:** We all mess up sometimes, and that's okay! Treat yourself like you would a friend who made a mistake. Learn from it and move on.

5. **Stay Flexible:** Things don't always go as planned, and that's okay! If something isn't working, try a different approach.

MINDFUL AWARENESS AND EMOTIONAL REGULATION

Do you ever wish you had the superpower to stay calm and collected no matter what life throws your way? Well, guess what? Mindfulness and emotional regulation might be the secret sauce you've been looking for! And this section will spill it out!

The Role of Mindfulness in Building Self-Control

Mindfulness isn't just about serene meditation sessions; it's a strong practice that makes you a super self-control master ready to navigate life's twists and turns with finesse. When you embrace mindfulness, you're giving your brain a superpower boost in the self-control department.

Here are some roles of mindfulness in building self-control:

- **Increased Awareness:** Mindfulness makes you aware of your thoughts, impulses, and emotions, allowing you to understand triggers for impulsive behaviors, and how to handle them.

- **Emotional Regulation:** By observing emotions without immediate reaction, mindfulness helps in managing intense feelings, reducing the likelihood of impulsive responses.
- **Reduced Stress:** Regular mindfulness practice reduces stress and anxiety, which are common triggers for impulsive behavior.
- **Improved Focus:** Mindfulness trains your mind to stay focused on the present moment, reducing distractions and enhancing your ability to stick to goals.
- **Enhanced Decision-Making:** By promoting a non-judgmental attitude, mindfulness helps in making balanced decisions rather than reacting impulsively based on immediate emotions.

Techniques for Managing Stress and Negative Emotions

By incorporating the techniques below into your routine, you can effectively manage stress and navigate negative emotions, promoting overall well-being and resilience.

- **Take Deep Breaths:** Did you ever notice how taking a deep breath can instantly make you feel better? It's not just a coincidence. Deep breathing is like hitting the reset button for your mind and body. So, when stress comes knocking, take a few slow, deep breaths and feel the tension melt away.
- **Find Your Zen Zone:** Your zen zone is that chill-out area you go to when you take a break from the world. Whether it's curling up with a good book on your bed, taking a relaxing bath, or spending time in nature, find what gives you peace and make time for it regularly. It's like giving yourself a mental hug!
- **Get Moving:** Exercise isn't just good for your physical health; it has a huge positive impact on your mental well-

being. Whether it's an early walk, a dance party in your living room, or a yoga session, moving your body releases feel-good chemicals in your brain that help you destress and boost your mood.

- **Ride the Wave:** Emotions come and go like ocean waves. Instead of trying to fight them, ride the wave instead. Acknowledge your feelings without judgment and remind yourself that they won't last forever. Be kind and permit yourself to feel the emotions. This can be incredibly liberating.
- **Practice Gratitude:** It's easy to get caught up in the whirlwind of stress and negativity, but focusing on the things you're grateful for can shift your perspective in a big way. Keep a gratitude journal, make a mental list before bed, or take a moment to appreciate the little good things in life.

Cultivating Self-Compassion and Resilience in the Face of Temptation

Do you always go hard on yourself when things go wrong? Well, it's time to flip the coin! Self-compassion is about treating yourself with the same kindness and understanding you would offer to a loved one. So, next time you face a tough decision, remember to be gentle with yourself. You're doing the best you can, and that's something to celebrate!

Resilience isn't about never experiencing setbacks; it's about bouncing back stronger than ever when life throws you a curveball. Think of it like a rubber band—you may get stretched but always snap back into shape. Cultivating resilience means embracing challenges as opportunities for growth, learning, and resilience-building. So, instead of viewing temptation as a roadblock, see it as a chance to flex your resilience muscles and emerge even stronger on the other side!

Just like any skill, you don't develop self-compassion and resilience overnight. Start by incorporating simple daily rituals into your routine, like writing down three things you're grateful for or offering yourself words of encouragement in moments of doubt. Over time, these small acts of self-compassion and resilience-building add up, helping you cultivate a deep well of inner strength to draw upon when temptation strikes.

BUILDING HEALTHY HABITS

We all create habits! You wake up in the morning, make your bed, brush your teeth, take your bath, and get ready to work, and you do this all weekdays. But why is it so hard to create healthy habits? That's because most of us are doing it the wrong way! In this section, we'll explore the science of habit formation, how to implement the habit loop for success, and tips to remain consistent.

The Science of Habit Formation

Have you ever wondered how effortlessly we slip into routines, almost as if on autopilot? It's all thanks to the fascinating science of habit formation.

Habits are like shortcuts—things you do without much thinking because you've done them many times. Also, habits are those things you've repeated regularly to the extent you find it hard to change. It can be anything from biting your nails, picking your lips, or eating healthy.

You might wonder, how do habits form? Our sensory nervous system is always looking for actions that will lead to dopamine release. As such, any new habit we develop results from our brain picking up on things that reward or punish us. When your brain picks a pattern, it stores that information in the basal ganglia, which is also in charge of emotions and memory. This may be the reason why habits are hard to break. They're formed in a brain region out of our control, so you're mostly unaware you're doing them (Mclachlan, 2021).

According to habit experts, the formation of habits follows a three-step loop: cue, routine, and reward (Raypole, 2020). First, there's the cue—a trigger that signals our brain to initiate a specific behavior. This could be anything from a familiar scent to a certain time of day or even an emotional state. Next comes the routine—the actual behavior itself. Whether reaching for a snack when feeling stressed or running after work, our brains automatically execute the routine in response to the cue. Finally, there's the reward—a positive outcome that reinforces the behavior and increases the likelihood of its repetition in the future.

Implementing Habit Loops for Long-Term Success

Ready to turn your goals into lasting habits? A good way to do that is by implementing the habit loop.

As mentioned above, the habit loop is divided into three steps—cue, routine, and reward. To implement habit loops effectively, start by identifying your current habits. What cues trigger them? What routines do you follow, and what rewards do you get? Understanding this will give you insight into your habits and what needs to change.

Let's say you want to replace a bad habit, like snacking on junk food, with a healthier one, like eating fruits. Identify the cue that triggers your snacking—stress or boredom. Instead of reaching for chips, have a bowl of fruit close by. The reward remains the same: satisfying your hunger or managing stress, but the routine changes to something healthier.

Creating new habits works the same way. Suppose you want to start exercising regularly. Choose a cue, like setting a specific time each day for your workout. Follow it with the exercise routine, and reward yourself afterward—maybe with a healthy snack, a relaxing shower, or simply the satisfaction of accomplishing your goal.

Remember, consistency is key. Repeating this loop strengthens your new habit over time. Start small. Tiny changes are easier to maintain and gradually build up into significant transformations. For instance, if you want to read more, start with just five minutes daily. As this becomes a habit, you can gradually increase the time.

So, how can habit loops push you to success? They do so by making your goals automatic. When your healthy routines become second nature, you free up mental energy to focus on bigger challenges. Imagine wanting to improve your skills at work. Instead of sporadically trying to learn new things, you establish a daily habit of reading industry news or taking online courses. The cue could be your morning coffee, the routine is the learning activity, and the reward is the satisfaction of gaining new knowledge.

Over time, these small, consistent actions accumulate, leading to significant personal and professional growth. Embedding success-oriented habits into your daily routine is like programming yourself for continuous improvement. The power of habit loops lies in their ability to create a stable foundation to build your dreams.

Tips for Overcoming Resistance and Maintaining Consistency

Sticking to new habits can be challenging, right? There are forces all around throwing setbacks, not to mention how hard it is to be consistent. Here are some simple, practical tips to help you overcome these hurdles and keep your new habits on track:

- **Use Reminders:** Visual or digital reminders can keep your new habits at the forefront of your mind. Set alarms, use sticky notes, or download a habit-tracking app. Reminders help reinforce your new routines until they become automatic.

- **Find Your Why:** Understanding why you want to develop a habit can boost your motivation. Reflect on why you started and how the change will improve your life. This deeper purpose can keep you going when motivation wanes.
- **Plan for Obstacles:** Things may not go as planned. Identify potential barriers and plan how to overcome them. If you know you'll be tired after work, schedule a morning workout instead. Having a plan B helps you stay on track.
- **Stay Accountable:** Share your goals with a friend or join a group with similar objectives. Accountability partners can provide support, encouragement, and a gentle nudge when you're feeling off track.
- **Be Kind to Yourself:** Everyone slips up occasionally; it's human. If you miss a day, don't be too hard on yourself. Acknowledge the slip-up, understand why it happened, and get back on track. Consistency over time is what truly matters.

Remember, building new habits takes time and effort. Be patient with yourself, keep pushing to resistance, and maintain consistency.

KEY TAKEAWAYS

- Self-control is like a muscle that develops with practice. Techniques such as setting clear goals, using reminders, understanding the deeper purpose behind our habits, and being kind to ourselves can help us maintain consistency and overcome resistance.
- Our brain's reward system drives instant gratification, prioritizing immediate pleasure over long-term rewards. Recognizing this tendency can help us develop strategies

to resist short-term temptations and focus on achieving long-term goals.

- Triggers and cues play a significant role in impulsive behaviors and habit formation. By identifying and understanding these triggers, we can modify our environment and routines to support healthier habits, quit bad habits, and have better self-control.

- Mindfulness and emotional regulation enhance self-control by helping us stay aware of impulses and effectively manage stress and negative emotions. These practices allow us to respond thoughtfully to challenges and focus on long-term objectives.

- The habit loop, consisting of cues, routine, and reward, is essential for forming and maintaining new habits. By being conscious of these loops, we can replace bad habits with positive ones and achieve long-term success through consistent actions.

In the next chapter, we'll discuss the link between self-discipline and self-compassion and how to cultivate the mindset of accepting yourself and prioritizing your well-being.

CHAPTER 5
NURTURING SELF-COMPASSION

Self-discipline is self-caring.

M. SCOTT PECK

Welcome to a chapter that is dear to my heart that focuses on an often overlooked yet crucial aspect of self-discipline: self-compassion. Many think being disciplined means being hard on yourself, but that's far from right. The key to real discipline lies in being kind and understanding toward yourself.

In this chapter, we'll explore how self-compassion can boost your self-discipline, debunk the myths that tell us self-criticism and perfectionism are the only ways to succeed, and learn how to embrace a mindset of kindness and acceptance. We'll also look at the importance of rest and self-care, setting boundaries, and overcoming those pesky self-sabotaging habits and limiting beliefs.

Get ready to discover how treating yourself with the same kindness you'd offer a loved one can transform your discipline and overall well-being.

THE IMPORTANCE OF SELF-COMPASSION

Picture yourself working hard toward a goal, pushing yourself to the limit, but despite your best efforts, you face a slip-up. What's your immediate reaction? You're not alone if it's harsh self-criticism or thoughts of not being good enough. Many believe being harsh on ourselves is the best way to achieve discipline and success. But what if I told you that the secret weapon is self-compassion?

Self-compassion is about treating yourself with the same kindness and understanding that you would offer a friend facing a tough time. It's recognizing that mistakes and setbacks are a natural part of the human experience, not a sign of personal failure. Studies have shown that self-compassion is strongly linked to higher optimism, happiness, and curiosity (Neff, 2009). When you're kind to yourself, you're more likely to bounce back from setbacks and stay committed to your goals. Dive in to know the link between self-discipline and self-compassion and debunk the myths about perfectionism.

Recognizing the Link Between Self-Compassion and Self-Discipline

Self-compassion and self-discipline seem like opposites. Self-discipline is often associated with strictness and pushing oneself hard, while self-compassion is about being gentle and forgiving with yourself. However, these two qualities can amazingly complement each other.

Self-compassion involves being kind to yourself, especially in times of difficulty and setbacks. When you approach your goals with self-compassion, you're more likely to stay motivated and less likely to burn out. Self-compassionate individuals are better at regulating their emotions and maintaining a balanced perspective. This emotional resilience supports sustained effort and perseverance—key components of self-discipline.

Think about a time you made a mistake. You might have felt discouraged and less motivated to try again if you responded with harsh self-criticism. In contrast, if you treated yourself with understanding and encouraged yourself to learn from the experience, you likely bounced back quicker and were more willing to keep pushing toward your goals. This is how self-compassion fuels self-discipline.

A study published on ResearchGate found that self-compassion can help reduce stress and improve self-regulation. Participants who practiced self-compassion reported higher levels of emotional well-being and were better able to manage their impulses and focus on their goals (Pepin et al., 2016).

Another excellent example of self-compassion blending with self-discipline is professional athletes. Many top performers, like Olympians, use self-compassion techniques to recover from setbacks. Instead of ruminating on their mistakes, they acknowledge them, learn from them, and move forward with stronger determination. This approach not only preserves their mental health but also enhances their performance by keeping their focus on improvement rather than perfection.

The balance between self-compassion and self-discipline is crucial for long-term success. When too hard on ourselves, we risk burnout and decreased motivation. However, pairing our goals with a compassionate approach fosters a healthier, more sustainable path to achievement. Self-compassion doesn't mean we slack off; instead, it means we're kind to ourselves as we achieve our goals. This kindness allows us to stay resilient and committed to our goals, making self-discipline more natural and enjoyable.

Dispelling Myths About Self-Criticism and Perfectionism

It's easy to think that self-criticism and perfectionism are necessary for success. However, these beliefs are more harmful than helpful.

Let's break down some common myths and understand the realities behind them.

Myth 1: Self-Criticism Is a Motivator

Many people believe that being hard on themselves will push them to achieve more. In reality, constant self-criticism can lead to decreased motivation and increased stress. You're more likely to feel defeated and give up when you're too critical. Instead, adopting a self-compassionate approach can enhance your motivation and resilience. For instance, rather than scolding yourself for a mistake, acknowledging it and focusing on improving can lead to better outcomes (Dee, 2017).

Myth 2: Perfectionism Leads to Excellence

Perfectionism is often seen as a pathway to excellence. However, striving for perfection mostly leads to procrastination and burnout. Perfectionists find it hard to do some tasks out of fear they won't meet their high standards. Moreover, they often need help completing tasks because they're never satisfied with the result. Embracing a "good enough" mentality can foster productivity and satisfaction. It's about progress, not perfection.

Myth 3: Perfectionists Have It All Together

There's a common perception that perfectionists are highly organized and entirely in control of their lives. The truth is that perfectionism is linked with anxiety and feelings of inadequacy. Perfectionists often focus more on their flaws and mistakes rather than their achievements. This mindset can lead to a constant state of stress and low self-esteem. Learning to accept imperfections and view mistakes as opportunities for growth can create a healthier and more balanced life (Martin, 2019).

Myth 4: Self-Criticism Helps Improve Performance

Some believe that criticizing oneself after a poor performance will lead to improvement. However, research suggests that self-compassion is a more practical approach. Being kind to yourself in the face of failure can reduce anxiety and improve your willingness to try again. This compassionate mindset encourages a learning attitude and resilience, which are crucial for long-term success.

Cultivating a Mindset of Kindness and Acceptance Toward Oneself

Developing a mindset of kindness and acceptance toward oneself is essential for overall well-being and happiness.

Self-acceptance means embracing all aspects of yourself—your strengths, weaknesses, and everything in between. It's about acknowledging your imperfections without judgment. By accepting yourself fully, you reduce the constant internal battle of trying to be someone you're not.

On the other hand, self-compassion involves being gentle and understanding with yourself, especially during tough times. Instead of harsh self-criticism, offer yourself words of encouragement and support. For example, if you make a mistake at work, instead of thinking, "I'm so stupid," try thinking, "Everyone makes mistakes. What can I learn from this?" This shift in thinking can help you build resilience and maintain a positive outlook.

Techniques for Cultivating Kindness and Acceptance

Incorporating the techniques below into your daily life can help you develop a more compassionate, understanding, and accepting approach to yourself and those around you:

- **Positive Affirmations:** Use positive affirmations to counteract negative self-talk like "I'm a failure" or "I can't do this." Phrases like "I'm enough" or "I deserve to be happy" can reinforce a positive self-image and boost self-esteem.

- **Indulge in Self-Care Practices:** Engage in activities that nurture your body and mind. This could include exercise, healthy eating, adequate sleep, and hobbies you enjoy. Taking care of your physical and mental health is a form of self-respect and kindness.
- **Try Journaling:** Writing about your thoughts and feelings can help you process emotions and develop a deeper understanding of yourself. It's a way to express self-compassion and track your growth over time.
- **Practice Gratitude:** Regularly reflecting on things you're grateful for can shift your focus from what's wrong to what's right in your life. Keeping a gratitude journal where you jot down a few things you're thankful for each day can significantly boost your mood and outlook.
- **Set boundaries:** Learn to say "no" to things that drain your energy and "yes" to things that uplift you. Setting boundaries is a form of self-care that ensures you're not overextending yourself and are prioritizing your well-being.

PRACTICING SELF-CARE AND REST

In the daily life marathon, where deadlines loom, and tasks pile up like an ever-growing mountain, rest isn't just a luxury; it's a necessity. Have you ever noticed how your productivity dwindles when running on empty? It's like trying to drive a car without refueling. To sustain peak performance, you need to replenish your reserves. This isn't just about physical energy but mental clarity, emotional resilience, and overall well-being. This section discusses the connection between rest, relaxation, and self-discipline. We'll also share strategies for incorporating self-care seamlessly into your routine.

The Role of Rest in Replenishing Self-Discipline Reserves

In today's fast-paced world, we all feel like we're running on fumes sometimes, with our energy levels plummeting and motivation waning. That's where the power of relaxation comes into play. It's not just about kicking back and doing nothing; it's about recharging your self-discipline batteries.

Think of self-discipline like a muscle that needs recovery time after intense use. Rest provides the necessary downtime to restore mental clarity, emotional resilience, and physical well-being. Even the most disciplined individuals can experience burnout and improved productivity during this recovery period.

Adequate rest improves cognitive function, enhances decision-making, and boosts overall performance (Diekelmann, 2014). It's not about being lazy; it's about working smarter by giving your mind and body the necessary breaks to function at their best. Rest isn't just about catching up on sleep (although that's crucial, too!). It encompasses activities that promote relaxation, reduce stress levels, and foster a sense of well-being.

Rest allows your muscles to repair and regenerate, reducing the risk of physical fatigue and injury. Activities like gentle stretching, yoga, or a leisurely walk can loosen tense muscles and improve blood circulation, enhancing overall vitality.

Have you ever noticed how solutions to problems often arise when you step away from them? Restorative activities like meditation, deep breathing exercises, or simply unplugging from screens can clear your head and promote creativity. Also, stress is a productivity killer. Taking time to relax helps regulate stress hormones like cortisol, fostering emotional resilience and improving your ability to handle challenges with a clear mind.

Some therapeutic activities that can help you unwind include light exercises like swimming or yoga and mindfulness techniques like progressive muscle relaxation (PMR) or guided imagery. Also, try to periodically unplug yourself from screens, especially before bed, to improve sleep quality.

Strategies for Incorporating Self-Care Activities Into Daily Routines

By implementing the following strategies, you can effectively incorporate self-care activities into your daily routine, enhancing your overall well-being and resilience.

1. **Start Small and Be Consistent:** Self-care doesn't have to be time-consuming or extravagant. Begin by dedicating just a few minutes daily to activities that recharge you. Consistency is key, whether it's enjoying a quiet cup of coffee in the morning, taking a short walk during lunch, or practicing deep breathing exercises before bed.

2. **Schedule Self-Care Time:** Treat self-care activities as non-negotiable appointments with yourself. Block out specific times in your daily schedule dedicated solely to self-care. This could be early in the morning before the day gets busy, during work breaks, or in the evening after the day's activities. By prioritizing these moments, you signal to yourself that your well-being matters.3.

3. **Identify Activities That Energize You:** Self-care is personal, so choose activities that make you feel centered and leave you feeling refreshed. These could be anything from reading a book to practicing yoga or meditation, cooking a healthy meal, or even indulging in a hobby you love. The goal is to engage in activities that uplift your spirits and replenish your energy levels.

4. **Mix Physical, Mental, and Emotional Care:** Self-care isn't limited to just one aspect of your well-being. Incorporate activities that nurture your physical, mental, and emotional health. For instance, combine a brisk walk outdoors (physical) with mindful breathing exercises (mental) and journaling about your feelings (emotional).

5. **Create a Self-Care Tool Kit:** Prepare for moments when you need a quick self-care boost. Fill your tool kit with items or activities that bring you comfort and relaxation, such as soothing music playlists, aromatherapy oils, a favorite book, or inspiring quotes. These readily available tools make it easier to practice self-care wherever you are.

Setting Boundaries and Prioritizing Personal Well-Being

Setting boundaries and prioritizing your well-being are like the guiding stars that keep you on track in the journey of self-discipline. They're not just about saying "no" or taking breaks—they're about consciously choosing how and what to invest your time and energy in to support your goals and overall happiness.

Setting boundaries means understanding your limits and communicating them effectively. It's about learning to say "no" when necessary without feeling guilty, whether declining extra projects at work or politely turning down social invitations to prioritize self-care.

Prioritizing your well-being goes hand in hand with setting boundaries. It involves recognizing when to step back and making intentional choices to nurture your physical, mental, and emotional health. This might mean scheduling regular exercise sessions, setting aside time for hobbies you enjoy, or ensuring you get enough sleep each night. These practices aren't selfish; they're essential for maintaining resilience and staying motivated in facing challenges.

OVERCOMING SELF-SABOTAGE AND LIMITING BELIEFS

Another important aspect of mastering self-discipline is overcoming self-sabotage and limiting beliefs.

Picture this: You have a goal—maybe starting your own business, getting fit, or learning a new skill. But as you get started, you find yourself procrastinating, doubting your abilities, and always getting distracted. These are signs of self-sabotage and limiting beliefs holding you back from reaching your full potential.

Self-sabotage can take many forms. It might be procrastination, negative self-talk, or even fear of success or failure. Limiting beliefs, on the other hand, are those ingrained thoughts that tell you what you can't do or aren't capable of achieving.

Overcoming self-sabotage and limiting beliefs is about challenging those inner voices and taking bold steps to change your mindset. It's about recognizing when you're holding yourself back and finding strategies to push through those barriers.

Identifying Self-Sabotaging Patterns and Negative Self-Talk

The first step to overcoming self-sabotaging and negative self-talk is understanding their pattern. Recognizing these patterns is crucial for improving self-discipline and achieving personal growth. Here are common self-sabotaging patterns:

1. **Procrastination:** This means delaying essential tasks or decisions, often due to fear of failure or perfectionism. Procrastination can stem from anxiety about not being able to meet high expectations.
2. **Self-Doubt:** This pattern is when you question your abilities, worth, or decisions. It can lead to indecision, or hesitating to take opportunities. Self-doubt can prevent individuals from taking necessary risks or pursuing ambitious goals.
3. **Perfectionism:** This involves setting excessively high standards that are difficult or impossible to meet, which can result in chronic dissatisfaction, stress, and fear of failure. Perfectionism can lead to procrastination and prevent individuals from completing tasks.

4. **Avoidance:** This pattern involves dodging challenges or responsibilities to evade discomfort or fear of failure. Avoidance can limit personal and professional growth by preventing individuals from confronting necessary difficulties.

On the other hand, negative self-talk involves critical or pessimistic internal dialogue that undermines self-confidence and motivation. Identifying and challenging negative self-talk is essential for improving self-esteem and fostering a positive mindset. Here are common forms of negative self-talk:

1. **All-or-Nothing Thinking:** Viewing situations in extreme terms, such as believing that any mistake makes you a complete failure. This type of thinking can be so unrealistic and damaging to self-esteem.
2. **Always Expecting the Worst:** Magnifying the importance or implications of adverse events or situations, often assuming the worst-case scenario will occur. This can lead to unnecessary anxiety and stress.
3. **Mind Reading:** Assuming you know what others think about you without evidence. This can contribute to social anxiety and self-consciousness.
4. **Self-Blame:** Blaming yourself excessively for external events or outcomes beyond your control. This pattern can lead to feelings of guilt or inadequacy.

Reframing Limiting Beliefs and Cultivating a Growth Mindset

Limiting beliefs are like invisible barriers holding you back from reaching your full potential. They often arise from past experiences, societal influences, or internalized fears. For example, if you've always believed you need to be more creative to pursue an art career, this belief may hinder you from exploring your artistic talents.

Here are some tips to help you reframe your limiting mindset:

- **Identify Your Limiting Beliefs:** Reflect on recurring thoughts that undermine your confidence or deter you from pursuing your goals. These could be beliefs about your abilities, worthiness, or potential for success.
- **Replace With Empowering Thoughts:** Replace negative self-talk with affirmations that assert your capabilities and potential. For instance, instead of thinking, "I'm not good enough," shift your mindset to "I'm continually improving and capable of achieving my goals."
- **Visualize Success:** Use visualization techniques to imagine overcoming challenges and achieving your desired outcomes. Visualization reinforces positive beliefs and strengthens your determination to pursue your goals.
- **Take Action:** Take conscious steps to overcome your limiting beliefs and work toward achieving your goals. Leave your comfort zone, take risks, and embrace new opportunities.

After reframing your limiting beliefs, the next step is to develop a growth mindset. A growth mindset is the belief that abilities and intelligence can be developed through dedication, effort, and perseverance. Unlike a fixed mindset that views talents and traits as static, a growth mindset thrives on challenges and sees failures as opportunities for learning and growth.

Here are practical strategies to cultivate a growth mindset:

- **Embrace Challenges:** Approach challenges with curiosity and optimism. See them as opportunities to stretch your skills and expand your knowledge.

- **Learn From Obstacles:** View setbacks as temporary and valuable learning experiences. Analyze what went wrong, identify lessons learned, and use that knowledge to improve your approach in the future.
- **Seek Feedback:** Welcome constructive feedback as a means to grow and develop. Seek advice and guidance from mentors, peers, or experts who can provide insights and suggestions for improvement.
- **Celebrate Progress:** Acknowledge and celebrate your efforts and achievements, no matter how small. Recognize that progress is a continuous journey, and each step forward contributes to your overall growth.

Harnessing the Power of Positive Affirmations and Visualization Technique

Other powerful tools we can utilize are the practice of positive affirmations and visualization techniques. These methods are instrumental in shaping our mindset and boosting our confidence toward achieving our goals.

Positive affirmations are like little pep talks to reinforce positive beliefs and attitudes. They can help counteract negative self-talk and cultivate a more optimistic outlook. Here are some tips to help you harness the power of positive affirmation:

- **Identify Key Affirmations:** Identify areas where you want to instill more confidence or positivity. For example, if you struggle with self-doubt in your abilities at work, your affirmation could be "I'm competent and capable of handling challenges."
- **Repetition Does Wonders:** Repeat your affirmations daily, preferably in the morning or before facing a challenging situation. Repetition helps embed these positive messages into your subconscious mind.

- **Believe in Your Words:** It's essential to genuinely believe in the affirmations you're repeating. They should resonate with your goals and aspirations, reinforcing your belief in your abilities.

Visualization involves mentally imagining yourself achieving your goals or performing at your best. It's a powerful technique used by successful individuals across various fields. Here's how you can effectively use visualization:

- **Create a Mental Image:** Close your eyes and imagine yourself succeeding in a specific task or achieving a desired outcome. Visualize the details—the sights, sounds, and emotions associated with your success.
- **Engage Your Senses:** Use all your senses to make the visualization as realistic as possible. Feel the excitement of accomplishing your goal, hear the applause or praise, and see yourself celebrating.
- **Practice Regularly:** Incorporate visualization into your daily routine before important events or challenges. Consistent practice enhances your confidence and mental readiness.

KEY TAKEAWAYS

- True self-discipline involves treating yourself with kindness and understanding, not harsh criticism. Self-compassion helps you bounce back from setbacks and stay committed to your goals.
- Self-compassion and discipline go hand in hand. Being kind to yourself enhances motivation, resilience, and emotional balance, which are crucial for achieving long-term goals.

- Self-criticism and perfectionism don't drive success; they often lead to stress and decreased motivation. Embracing self-compassion fosters healthier motivation and a focus on progress over perfection.
- Practices like mindfulness, positive affirmations, self-care, and setting boundaries nurture self-esteem, emotional well-being, and sustained self-discipline.

In the next chapter, we'll discuss how to strengthen your willpower, how to set and maintain boundaries, and how to draw inspiration from role models and success stories.

CHAPTER 6
STRENGTHENING WILLPOWER

Willpower is like a muscle: the more you train it, the stronger it gets.

UNKNOWN

Willpower is the driving force behind achieving your goals and overcoming setbacks. It's that inner strength that helps you resist temptations, stay focused on your long-term objectives, and push through challenging times. But just like a muscle, it can get tired and worn out if overused without proper care. Understanding and strengthening your willpower can significantly impact your ability to stay disciplined and achieve your dreams.

In this chapter, we'll explore willpower depletion and how to manage it effectively. We'll also look into ego depletion and how decision fatigue can drain your mental resources. Moreover, we'll dive into strategies to conserve and replenish your willpower and how creating the right environment can help preserve your mental stamina.

Next, we'll discuss how to build your willpower reserves, the importance of self-awareness, and how setting boundaries can help manage your willpower. You'll also learn about innovative techniques like temptation bundling and reward systems that make reinforcing willpower easier and more enjoyable.

Finally, we'll look into the powerful forces of motivation and inspiration. Discovering your "why" and harnessing intrinsic motivation can provide a strong foundation for willpower. We'll also explore how cultivating a growth mindset and embracing challenges can strengthen your resolve and how inspiration from role models and success stories can keep you motivated.

By the end of this chapter, you'll have a tool kit of strategies to strengthen your willpower, manage its depletion, and maintain the motivation needed to pursue your goals with renewed energy and unmatched determination.

UNDERSTANDING WILLPOWER DEPLETION

Have you ever noticed how making decisions all day can mentally exhaust you? That's willpower depletion in action. Your brain's energy tank is running empty, making it harder to resist temptations and focus on your goals. In this section, we'll explore what willpower depletion is and how you can manage it to keep your inner strength intact.

The concept of willpower depletion, often called "ego depletion," suggests that our self-control is a finite resource. Just like a muscle gets tired after heavy use, our willpower can drain after making numerous decisions or resisting multiple temptations throughout the day. This can lead to decision fatigue, where our ability to make good choices diminishes, and we become more prone to impulsive actions.

But don't worry, it's not all doom and gloom! Understanding this concept is the first step to managing it effectively. There are strategies you can employ to conserve and replenish your willpower, and that's exactly what this section will cover!

We'll also discuss how you can create environments that support willpower preservation. This means setting up your surroundings to minimize temptations and distractions.

By the end of this section, you'll have a clearer understanding of how willpower works and practical tips to manage its depletion. This knowledge will empower you to make better decisions, resist temptations more effectively, and stay on track toward achieving your goals with greater ease and resilience.

The Concept of Ego Depletion and Decision Fatigue

There were times when we all felt completely drained after a day filled with endless decisions. That's ego depletion at work. The concept of ego depletion suggests that our ability to exert self-control and make decisions is a limited resource that can be exhausted over time. Picture this as a battery; each decision you make throughout the day drains a bit of that battery until, eventually, you're running on empty.

Ego depletion and decision fatigue are interconnected concepts that show how our mental resources can be exhausted over time, particularly through decision-making and self-control tasks.

Ego depletion refers to the idea that self-control or willpower draws upon a limited pool of mental resources that can be used up. When you use a lot of willpower on one task, you have less available for subsequent tasks. This depletion can make you more likely to give in to temptations or make impulsive decisions. For instance, after a long day of making difficult decisions at work, you might find it harder to resist that piece of cake or stick to your evening exercise routine.

For example, a study found that people who exert a lot of self-control in one area are more likely to give in to temptations in another (Pignatiello et al., 2018). If you've been holding back from snacking all day, you might find yourself giving in and eating a large, unhealthy meal at night.

Decision fatigue, on the other hand, describes the deteriorating quality of decisions an individual makes after a lengthy decision-making session. The more choices you make throughout the day, the harder each one becomes for your brain, and eventually, it looks for shortcuts. This can lead to impulsive decisions, avoidance of decisions, or opting for the easiest rather than the best options. For example, judges are more likely to grant parole early in the day and after breaks when their decision-making resources are less depleted.

Research has shown that individuals experiencing decision fatigue show an impaired ability to make trade-offs, mostly prefer to be passive in decision-making, and are more likely to make irrational choices (Pignatiello et al., 2018b).

Strategies for Conserving and Replenishing Willpower

There are effective strategies to conserve and replenish your willpower, ensuring you can stay on track with your goals and not experience ego depletion. Here are some practical approaches to managing your willpower:

1. **Get Enough Sleep:** Sleep is essential for replenishing willpower. When you're well-rested, your brain can better manage self-control and decision-making. Aim for 7-8 hours of quality sleep each night to keep your willpower reserves high.
2. **Get Physical:** Physical activity boosts physical health and enhances mental stamina. Regular exercise increases overall energy and reduces stress, which in turn helps conserve willpower.
3. **Break Tasks Into Smaller Chunks:** Tackling large tasks can quickly drain willpower. Breaking them into smaller, manageable steps makes them less daunting and conserves your mental energy. Celebrate small wins to stay motivated.

4. **Limit Decision-Making:** Reduce the number of decisions you have to make daily. This can be done by planning your day, setting routines, and automating decisions like meal choices or outfits. Fewer decisions mean less decision fatigue.

5. **Take Regular Breaks:** Short breaks throughout the day can help restore mental energy. The Pomodoro Technique, which involves working for 25 minutes and then taking a 5-minute break, is a great way to maintain productivity and willpower.

6. **Stay Positive:** Positive thinking and self-affirmation can boost your willpower. Encouraging yourself and focusing on your strengths can help you overcome challenges more effectively

7. **Manage Stress:** Chronic stress quickly depletes willpower. Finding ways to manage stress, such as through hobbies, relaxation techniques, or professional help, can protect your mental resources.

Creating Environments Conducive to Willpower Preservation

One of the most effective ways to strengthen your willpower is to create an environment that supports your goals. When your surroundings are set up to reduce temptations and distractions, you'll find it much easier to stay on track. Here are some tips to help you design an environment conducive to willpower preservation:

1. **Organize Your Space:** A clutter-free environment can help clear your mind and reduce stress. Organize your workspace, remove unnecessary items, and create a dedicated area for focus and productivity. A tidy space leads to a tidy mind, making concentrating and exerting self-control easier.

2. **Do Away With Temptations:** Identify the things that frequently distract you or lead you off course and remove them from your immediate environment. For example, if you can't stop browsing social media, consider using website blockers during work hours.

3. **Create Routines and Habits:** Establishing routines can automate your actions, reducing the need for willpower. Simple habits like planning your day the night before, setting specific times for breaks, or having a regular exercise schedule make your daily tasks feel more manageable and less draining on your willpower.

4. **Use Visual Cues:** Visual reminders of your goals can keep you motivated. This might include vision boards, motivational quotes, or just writing your goals in a journal and keeping them beside your bed. These cues can serve as gentle reminders to stay on track.

5. **Control Your Environment:** Sometimes, changing your environment is necessary. This could mean working in a quieter space if your home is noisy or finding a study group if you need accountability. Tailor your surroundings to support the behaviors you want to encourage.

BUILDING WILLPOWER RESERVES

This section focuses on building willpower reserves, an essential skill supporting long-term success and resilience.

Earlier, we described willpower as like muscle: With the right exercises and habits, it can be made stronger and more enduring.

First, we'll explore the role of self-awareness in managing willpower. Self-awareness helps you understand what depletes your willpower and how to counteract these drains effectively. Recognizing your triggers and patterns allows you to anticipate and prepare for challenges. We'll share techniques for setting and maintaining boundaries, and finally, we'll round up with how to use temptation bundling and reward systems to reinforce willpower.

The Role of Self-Awareness in Managing Willpower

Self-awareness plays an essential role in managing and enhancing your willpower. Think of it as your internal compass, guiding you through the ups and downs of maintaining self-discipline.

Being self-aware means understanding your triggers and patterns that lead to willpower depletion. For instance, you might notice that you're more likely to indulge in unhealthy snacks when stressed or tired. Recognizing this pattern is the first step in setting up strategies to avoid unhealthy eating. Preparing healthy snacks ahead of time or ensuring you get adequate sleep are proactive measures that can reduce tiredness, thus saving you from unhealthy eating.

Moreover, self-awareness helps you pinpoint your peak performance times. You might discover that your willpower is strongest in the morning, making it the ideal time to tackle challenging tasks. Conversely, if your resolve weakens in the evening, you can plan less demanding activities or establish a calming evening routine to preserve willpower.

Mindfulness is another aspect of self-awareness that's crucial in managing willpower. Mindfulness enhances your ability to observe your impulses without immediately acting on them, allowing you to make thoughtful decisions instead of impulsive ones. This practice can significantly bolster your willpower by helping you control your actions.

Self-awareness also involves understanding your values and goals, which keeps you motivated and aligned with what truly matters to you. When you're clear about why you want to achieve something, harnessing the willpower needed to stay committed becomes easier. Knowing your goals and values also helps maintain focus and motivation, making it simpler to summon the willpower required for long-term success.

In essence, self-awareness is the foundation for effectively managing your willpower. By understanding your habits, leveraging mindfulness, aligning with your core values, and recognizing when to rest, you can build a sustainable approach to self-discipline. This helps you achieve your goals and maintain a healthy balance in your life.

Techniques for Setting and Maintaining Boundaries

By implementing the techniques below, you can effectively set and maintain healthy boundaries that protect your well-being and promote respectful interactions.

- **Know Your Limits:** Regularly check in with yourself to understand your physical, emotional, and mental limits. Self-awareness helps you recognize what you can and can't tolerate, ensuring you don't overextend yourself. For instance, if you notice feeling drained after certain activities, it's a sign to reassess your involvement in them.
- **Communicate Clearly:** Use assertive yet respectful language to communicate your needs and limits to others. Clear communication can prevent misunderstandings and ensure that your boundaries are respected. For example, if a coworker frequently interrupts you, you might say, "I need to focus on this project for the next hour. Can we discuss this later?"
- **Consistency:** Once you've set a boundary, consistently enforce it. This consistency helps others understand and respect your limits. For instance, if you decide not to check work emails after 7 pm, stick to this rule, even if it means explaining to colleagues or clients that you'll respond the next day.

- **Learn to Say "No":** Practice saying "no" politely and firmly. This helps you avoid overcommitting and gives you enough time and energy for your priorities. For example, if a friend asks for help with a project but your schedule is full, you could respond, "I'd love to help, but I'm really busy this week. Can we make it another time?"
- **Prioritize Self-Care:** Schedule regular self-care activities to replenish your energy. This could include hobbies, exercise, or simply relaxing. Ensuring you have time for self-care helps maintain your overall well-being and prevents burnout. For example, setting aside time for a daily walk or a weekly hobby can significantly improve your mood and energy levels.
- **Adjust as Needed:** Regularly reassess your boundaries to ensure they continue to meet your needs. Life circumstances change, and so should your boundaries. For instance, if your current work-life balance isn't working, take steps to adjust it, such as setting stricter work hours or delegating more tasks.

Using Temptation Bundling and Reward Systems to Reinforce Willpower

Combining activities you love with less enjoyable tasks, a strategy known as temptation bundling, dramatically enhances your willpower.

What is temptation bundling? This technique involves pairing an activity you enjoy with one you need to do but might not find appealing. By linking the two, you make the less desirable task more enjoyable. For example, you could only watch your favorite show while exercising. This way, you're more likely to stick to your exercise routine because it's tied to something you look forward to.

On the other hand, reward systems involve implementing a reward system that can bolster your willpower. Setting up small rewards for accomplishing tasks creates positive reinforcement that encourages you to keep going. For instance, after completing a challenging project, you might treat yourself to a nice dinner or a fun activity. These rewards can be immediate or delayed, but the key is that they should be something you genuinely look forward to.

Practical Examples of Temptation Bundling

1. **Listening to Audiobooks During Chores:** If you dislike doing household chores, listen to an engaging audiobook or podcast while you work. This makes the chore more enjoyable and helps you stay motivated to complete it.
2. **Sweet Treats After Tasks:** If you have a sweet tooth, reward yourself with a small treat after completing a challenging task. This immediate reward boosts your motivation and makes the task less monotonous.
3. **Social Activities Post-Work:** After a productive day, plan fun activities with friends or family. Knowing that you plan something enjoyable can motivate you to complete your work more efficiently.

Using temptation bundling and reward systems makes challenging tasks more enjoyable and helps you build and sustain your willpower. It's a practical and effective way to boost your productivity and achieve your goals without feeling overwhelmed.

Harnessing Motivation and Inspiration

Have you ever wondered why some tasks feel effortless while others drain you? It's about finding your "why"—the deep-seated reason behind your actions that keeps you going, even when it gets tricky.

Imagine facing challenges not with reluctance but with excitement, seeing each hurdle as a chance to grow and improve. That's the essence of cultivating a growth mindset—believing your abilities can develop through effort and perseverance. It's about embracing challenges as opportunities for personal evolution and skill enhancement.

The next section will explore how uncovering your "why" and tapping into your intrinsic motivation can propel you forward. We'll also discuss how to draw inspiration from role models and success stories.

Finding Your "Why" and Tapping Into Intrinsic Motivation

Understanding your "why" is like uncovering the compass that guides you through life's journey. It's that deep-rooted reason behind your actions; the driving force that fuels your passion and determination from within. Instead of merely trying to achieve your goals, knowing your "why" gives every task, goal, and endeavor a sense of purpose and meaning.

Tapping into your intrinsic motivation means connecting with what truly matters to you personally. It's about finding joy, satisfaction, and fulfillment in the process itself rather than relying solely on results or pressures. For example, if you're passionate about helping others, your "why" might be the desire to positively impact people's lives, regardless of recognition or financial gain.

Research indicates that intrinsic motivation enhances productivity and overall well-being. When intrinsically motivated, you're more likely to persist in facing challenges because the work aligns with your values and brings you genuine satisfaction (Marinoff, 2019). This internal drive also fosters creativity, innovation, and a deeper sense of engagement with your goals.

To discover your "why," take time for introspection. Reflect on moments in your life when you felt most fulfilled or energized. Consider activities or goals that bring you a sense of joy and purpose. Your "why" might evolve as you gain new experiences and insights, but it remains a consistent source of motivation that anchors you during uncertain times.

Once you identify your "why," try integrating it into your daily life and letting it guide your decisions, prioritize activities that align with your core values, and seek opportunities that allow you to express your passion. By nurturing your intrinsic motivation, you cultivate a deeper connection to your goals and greater fulfillment in everything you pursue.

Ultimately, finding your "why" is about understanding yourself more deeply and aligning your actions with what truly inspires and drives you. It empowers you to approach challenges with resilience, creativity, and a profound sense of purpose, making your journey toward success more meaningful and rewarding.

Drawing Inspiration From Role Models and Success Stories

Have a mentor whose journey deeply connects with your ambitions and dreams. Role models and success stories offer more than just inspiration; they present a roadmap of possibilities and a wellspring of motivation to drive you toward your objectives.

Role models are individuals who embody qualities or achievements that you admire and wish to emulate. They can be from any walk of life—athletes, entrepreneurs, artists, scientists, or even someone within your community. The key is identifying traits or accomplishments in them that resonate with your values and aspirations.

When you draw inspiration from role models, you tap into their experiences, wisdom, and strategies for success. Their stories often highlight resilience in adversity, perseverance through challenges, and the courage to pursue ambitious goals. Learning from their journeys gives you valuable insights and guidance to inform your path.

Success stories, on the other hand, provide tangible evidence of what's possible when dedication, passion, and hard work converge. Whether it's reading about a start-up that overcame initial failures to achieve global success or an athlete who shattered records through unwavering commitment, these narratives illustrate the power of persistence and determination.

Exposure to role models and success stories can significantly impact motivation and goal achievement. Witnessing others' accomplishments can boost self-efficacy—believing one can succeed in specific situations. This heightened confidence can inspire you to set higher goals, overcome obstacles with resilience, and stay committed to your vision.

By drawing inspiration from role models and success stories, you cultivate a mindset of possibility and achievement and harness the motivation needed to navigate your path toward success. They serve as beacons of hope and proof that anything is attainable with dedication, resilience, and a clear vision.

KEY TAKEAWAYS

- Willpower acts like a muscle that can deplete after making numerous decisions or resisting temptations throughout the day. This depletion, known as ego depletion, can lead to decision fatigue, making it harder to maintain self-control and make good choices.
- Practical strategies for replenishing your willpower include getting enough sleep, eating healthy, engaging in physical activity, practicing mindfulness, breaking tasks into smaller chunks, limiting decision-making, taking regular breaks, staying positive, seeking support, and managing stress.
- Tailoring your environment to minimize distractions and temptations can significantly support willpower. This involves organizing your space, removing temptations, establishing routines, using visual cues, controlling your environment, and leveraging positive influences from supportive networks.

- Self-awareness is key to managing willpower effectively. Understanding your triggers, setting boundaries, and using techniques like temptation bundling and reward systems can help build and sustain willpower over time.

In the next chapter, we'll take a look at the psychology of procrastination, the role of fear and perfectionism, and how to cultivate a procrastination-proof mindset.

CHAPTER 7
OVERCOMING PROCRASTINATION

Procrastination is like a credit card: it's a lot of fun until you get the bill.

CHRISTOPHER PARKER

We've all been there: putting off important tasks until the pressure mounts and stress kicks in. But procrastination isn't just about time management; it's deeply rooted in our psychology. Understanding why we procrastinate and adopting effective strategies can liberate us from this cycle.

In this chapter, we'll explore the psychology behind procrastination. Fear of failure and perfectionism often hold us back, while analysis paralysis and decision avoidance can keep us stuck. By uncovering these patterns, we can begin to dismantle them.

We'll also dive into practical strategies for beating procrastination. From breaking tasks into smaller steps to leveraging time-blocking and the 2-minute rule, these techniques empower us to take action and stay focused.

Let's start our journey to overcome procrastination. Together, we'll uncover insights and tools to reclaim our productivity and achieve our goals with greater ease and satisfaction.

UNDERSTANDING THE PSYCHOLOGY OF PROCRASTINATION

Ever wondered why putting off tasks seems easier than tackling them head-on? Let's peel back the layers of procrastination and understand what makes us delay. From fearing failure to chasing perfection and getting stuck in decision limbo, we'll unlock the psychology of procrastination.

The Root Causes of Procrastination and Avoidance Behavior

Procrastination and avoidance are like those pesky chores we keep putting off. We've all been there, staring at a task we know we must do and even running out of deadlines but somehow finding a hundred other things to do instead. The big question is why we do this and what lies beneath these behaviors.

Simply put, procrastination is the art of delaying or postponing something that needs to be done. Whether it's a work assignment, cleaning the house, or starting a new project, procrastination sneaks in when we avoid tackling tasks head-on. It's not just about poor time management; it often runs deeper, tapping into our emotions and thoughts.

Avoidance behavior is very similar to procrastination; it involves dodging tasks or situations that make us uncomfortable or anxious. This could be avoiding difficult conversations, ignoring responsibilities, or delaying decisions. Avoidance gives us temporary relief from discomfort, but it can trap us in a cycle of delaying things we face sooner or later.

Now, let's dig into why we procrastinate and avoid certain tasks:

- **Fear of Failure:** This is a big one. The fear of not doing something perfectly or of failing can paralyze us. It's like our mind protects us from disappointment or criticism. So, instead of risking failure, you delay starting the task altogether.
- **Perfectionism:** Have you ever waited for the perfect moment or idea before starting? That's perfectionism at play. People who set such high standards for themselves find it challenging to begin a task. You might procrastinate because you're waiting for conditions to be just right—which, let's face it, rarely happens.
- **Avoidance of Discomfort:** Tasks that trigger uncomfortable emotions like anxiety, boredom, or frustration are often avoided. It's easier to procrastinate than to confront these feelings directly. Whether it's a daunting project or a challenging conversation, avoidance keeps us from facing uncomfortable situations.
- **Feeling Overwhelmed:** Large tasks or projects can feel overwhelming, making it difficult to know where to start. This feeling of overwhelm can lead to procrastination as we avoid diving into something that seems too complex. Breaking tasks into smaller, manageable steps can make them more approachable.

The Role of Fear of Failure and Perfectionism

Have you ever caught yourself putting off a task because you're worried it won't turn out perfectly? Or do you delay starting something because you're afraid of failing? Let's explore how fear of failure and perfectionism influence our tendency to procrastinate.

The fear of not meeting expectations, disappointing others, or making mistakes can be paralyzing. This fear often stems from past experiences where failure led to negative consequences, such as criticism, rejection, or a sense of personal inadequacy. As a result, you might avoid a task altogether or delay starting it. This avoidance provides temporary relief from the anxiety associated with potential failure but ultimately leads to increased stress as deadlines approach. This is fear of failure.

For example, if you have a presentation to prepare for work, you might put it off until the last minute because you're afraid of not delivering a flawless performance. The fear of stumbling over your words or not impressing your colleagues holds you back from taking the initial steps needed to prepare adequately.

Perfectionism is another significant factor that contributes to procrastination. It involves setting excessively high standards for yourself and your work. You may delay starting a task because you want everything to be perfect. This desire for perfection can manifest in different ways, such as spending excessive time planning, researching, or revising before executing the task.

For instance, you're tasked with writing a report. You might spend hours researching every detail and meticulously outlining the structure, striving for perfection in each section. However, this meticulous preparation can lead to procrastination if you fixate on getting everything right before progressing to the writing phase.

Both fear of failure and perfectionism create psychological barriers that hinder productivity and progress. They can lead to a cycle of avoidance where tasks are postponed or avoided altogether due to the anxiety and pressure of not meeting high standards or expectations.

By acknowledging the fear of failure, you can reframe mistakes as opportunities for growth rather than personal shortcomings. Embracing a growth mindset allows you to view challenges as learning experiences that contribute to your development and resilience.

Similarly, addressing perfectionism involves setting realistic goals and expectations for yourself. It's about recognizing that perfection is unattainable and that progress and completion are more important than flawless outcomes. By focusing on consistent action and making incremental improvements, you can overcome the paralysis that perfectionism often induces.

Overcoming Analysis Paralysis and Decision Avoidance

Many of us struggle with something we don't know: analysis paralysis and decision avoidance. These two terms sound technical, but they describe situations that are very familiar and happen in our day-to-day activities.

Have you ever been stuck overthinking a decision to the point where you can't make a choice? Or you may avoid making decisions altogether because it feels too overwhelming. If this sounds familiar, you're not alone!

Analysis paralysis happens when you overthink a decision so much that you can't move forward. Envisage you're trying to choose a new smartphone. You start by researching different models, reading reviews, comparing specs, and watching YouTube videos. Hours turn into days and days into weeks, but you still need to decide. This is analysis paralysis—there's too much information available that makes a choice overwhelming, leaving you feeling stuck and unable to make a choice.

Decision avoidance, on the other hand, is when you dodge making a choice because it feels too stressful or complicated. For example, you might decide to move to a new city for a job. Instead of weighing the pros and cons and choosing, you put it off, hoping that the right choice will become obvious. This avoidance can lead to missed opportunities and increased stress as the decision hangs over you.

Tips to Overcome Analysis Paralysis and Decision Avoidance

By implementing the tips below, you can overcome analysis paralysis and decision avoidance, making more timely and confident decisions.

1. **Set Clear Deadlines:** One of the best ways to combat analysis paralysis is to set a clear deadline for making your decision. For example, if you're trying to decide on a new phone, give yourself a week to gather information and then commit to deciding by the end of that week. This helps prevent endless searches and forces you to take action.

2. **Limit Your Options:** Too many choices can be overwhelming. Try to narrow down your options to a manageable number. For instance, if you're planning a vacation, limit your choices to three places that fit your criteria instead of considering every destination in the world. This makes the decision-making process more manageable.

3. **Use the 80/20 Rule:** The 80/20 rule, also known as the Pareto Principle, suggests that 80% of results come from 20% of efforts. Apply this to decision-making by focusing on the most important factors influencing your decision. For example, when buying a car, prioritize key aspects like reliability and fuel efficiency rather than getting bogged down by every minor feature.

4. **Trust Your Instincts:** While gathering information is important, consider the value of your gut feeling. If you're torn between two options, ask yourself which one you're naturally more drawn to. Often, your initial instinct indicates what will make you happiest in the long run.

5. **Accept Imperfection:** Remember that no decision is perfect. Every choice has pros and cons, and predicting every outcome is impossible. Accepting this can alleviate some of the pressure you feel to make the "perfect" choice. Focus on making a well-informed decision rather than a flawless one.

Strategies for Beating Procrastination

Let's discuss some simple yet effective strategies to beat procrastination. We all know how tempting it is to put things off, but with a few easy tricks, you can stay on top of your tasks and boost productivity. What are these simple yet effective strategies? Keep reading!

Breaking Tasks Down Into Smaller Manageable Steps

Breaking tasks into smaller, manageable steps is a game-changer for tackling big projects without feeling overwhelmed or procrastinating. Let's look at some practical ways to do this effectively.

First, start by identifying your main goal or project. Once you have that clear, break it down into smaller tasks. For example, if you need to organize an event, list all the components: booking the venue, sending invitations, arranging catering, etc. Each becomes a smaller task you can tackle one at a time.

Next, prioritize these tasks. Determine which ones need to be done first and which can wait. This helps you focus on what's most important right now and prevents you from getting bogged down by less critical tasks. For instance, booking the venue might be your top priority, while choosing the menu can come later.

Another tip is to set deadlines for each smaller task. This keeps you on track and creates a sense of urgency. Use a calendar or a project management tool to schedule these deadlines, ensuring you allocate enough time for each step. For instance, you might decide to book the venue by the end of the week and finalize the guest list by the end of the month.

Visual aids can also be incredibly helpful. Creating a checklist or a flowchart can give you a clear overview of what needs to be done and help you track your progress. For example, a flowchart for planning an event can show you which tasks depend on others, making it easier to see the sequence of actions required.

Lastly, be flexible and adjust your plan as needed. Sometimes, things are unexpected, and you might need to re-prioritize tasks or adjust deadlines. Staying adaptable ensures that you can handle any surprises without getting too stressed.

By breaking down tasks into smaller, manageable steps, prioritizing, setting deadlines, using visual aids, celebrating small wins, and staying flexible, you can make even the most daunting projects feel achievable.

Utilizing Time-Blocking and Deadlines to Create Momentum

Time-blocking is all about scheduling specific blocks of time for different tasks throughout your day. Instead of multitasking, you dedicate a focused period to a single task. Imagine blocking out 9-10 am for checking emails, 10 am to 12 pm for project work, and 1-2 pm for meetings. This method helps you stay organized and allocate time to all your essential tasks.

Setting deadlines works hand in hand with time-blocking. Deadlines create a sense of urgency and help you stay committed to your schedule. For instance, if you block out time for writing a report, set a deadline to complete the first draft by the end of the week. This keeps you accountable and breaks down large tasks into manageable chunks, making them less intimidating.

When you combine time-blocking with deadlines, you create a powerful system that keeps you focused and motivated. Start by planning your day or week, blocking out time for each task, and setting realistic deadlines. This structure helps you stay on track and make consistent progress.

Let's break it down with an example. Suppose you have a big presentation to prepare for. Instead of trying to do everything at once, you block out specific times over the week: Monday morning for research, Tuesday afternoon for drafting slides, and Wednesday evening for practicing your delivery. Each session has a clear goal, and by the end of the week, you've made steady progress without feeling overwhelmed.

Another benefit of time-blocking is that it helps you identify and eliminate time-wasters. When you see your schedule laid out, it becomes clear where you might be spending too much time on low-priority tasks. Adjusting your blocks accordingly can help you focus more on what truly matters.

To make time-blocking even more effective, use tools like calendars or apps. Digital calendars can send reminders and help you stick to your schedule. Remember to include breaks in your schedule. Working nonstop can lead to burnout, so block time for short breaks and lunch. This helps you recharge and maintain productivity throughout the day. For example, after a focused 90-minute work block, take a 10-minute break to stretch or grab a coffee. This can refresh your mind and improve your overall efficiency.

Implementing the 2-minute Rule and Other Productivity Hacks

Ever heard of the 2-minute rule? It's a simple yet powerful productivity hack that can help you tackle those small tasks that often pile up. The idea is straightforward: If a task takes two minutes or less to complete, do it immediately. This could be anything from replying to an email to filing a document or even doing a quick chore. Handling these quick tasks right away prevents them from becoming larger, more daunting tasks later on.

The beauty of the 2-minute rule lies in its simplicity. It's amazing how many little things we put off that can be done in a flash. For example, you might notice a messy desk but think you'll clean it later. Instead, if it only takes a couple of minutes, do it now. You'll be surprised at how much tidier and more organized your workspace and mind feel afterward.

But the 2-minute rule is just the start. Other productivity hacks can also make a big difference. One popular technique is the 5-minute rule. Like the 2-minute rule, it's about getting started on a task you've procrastinated on. Commit to working on it for just five minutes. Often, the hardest part is starting, and once you're in the flow, you'll find it easier to continue.

Batching tasks is another effective strategy. Group similar tasks together and tackle them in one go. For example, set aside specific times of the day to respond to emails instead of checking them constantly. This way, you minimize the time lost to switching between different types of tasks and stay in a more productive flow.

KEY TAKEAWAYS

- Procrastination often stems from psychological factors like fear of failure, perfectionism, and avoidance of discomfort. Recognizing these triggers can help you address them effectively.
- Dividing large projects into smaller, manageable steps makes them more manageable. Prioritize tasks, set deadlines, and use visual aids to track progress and maintain momentum.
- Utilize time-blocking to organize your day, set clear deadlines to create urgency, and use the 2-minute rule to tackle quick tasks immediately. These strategies can significantly boost productivity and reduce procrastination.

In the next chapter, we'll discuss the importance of consistency in achieving long-term goals, staying motivated and avoiding burnout, and reviewing and adjusting your goals.

CHAPTER 8
SUSTAINING LONG-TERM SUCCESS

The secret of your success is determined by your daily agenda.

JOHN C. MAXWELL

You finish a marathon and feel great about it. Now, you're thinking: Should I celebrate quickly or start preparing for future races to keep up my improved fitness? This situation reflects the importance of long-term success. While achieving a big goal is exciting, the real challenge is maintaining that success over time.

This chapter is all about keeping that momentum alive and running. We'll explore how consistency plays a vital role in reaching your long-term goals and how to stay motivated without burning out. We'll also look at the importance of reflection and feedback. Regularly reviewing your progress helps you see how far you've come and identifies areas where you can improve.

Finally, we'll examine the balance between consistency and flexibility. While sticking to your plans is important, life can be unpredictable. Being able to adapt your goals and strategies in response to changing circumstances is key to maintaining long-term success.

Ready to transform your achievements into lasting success? Let's dive into it!

MAINTAINING MOMENTUM

You've set goals, made some initial progress, and are riding the wave of success. But how do you keep that momentum going? It's like trying to keep a kite flying high in the sky—once you've got it up there, you must manage the wind, adjust your string, and stay attentive to keep it soaring. This section is about ensuring your kite doesn't come crashing down, but this is a kite of goals!

Let's explore why sticking to a routine and maintaining consistent actions are crucial for sustained success. We'll dive into strategies that keep your enthusiasm alive and help you avoid burnout. That's not all; we'll also look at how to overcome plateaus and adapt to setbacks.

The Importance of Consistency in Achieving Long-Term Goals

Consistency might be the most underrated secret to success. Imagine if a runner only trained sporadically or a musician only practiced their instrument occasionally. Progress would be slow, and reaching goals would feel like a distant dream. The same principle applies to all our personal and professional goals.

When we talk about consistency, we're talking about regular, repeated actions that lead to progress over time. It's like planting a garden: You need to water the plants daily, not just when you remember or feel like it. This steady effort builds a foundation that makes achieving our goals much more attainable.

One major reason consistency is crucial is that it helps build momentum. Small, regular actions compound, creating an effect that propels us forward. Each step, no matter how tiny, adds up. Before you know it, these small actions turn into significant achievements. It's not about making huge leaps every day but about making sure you're making a move every day.

Moreover, consistency helps in developing habits. When you do something regularly, it becomes second nature. This reduces the mental effort needed to perform the task, making it easier to stick with your plans even when motivation wanes.

But let's not forget the confidence boost that comes with consistency. When you see progress from your efforts, no matter how small, it reinforces your belief in your abilities. This confidence fuels further action, creating positive feedback that keeps you going and hungry for achievements.

Consistency also provides a sense of stability and predictability in our lives. It allows us to create routines that make managing our time and energy easier. For instance, having a consistent morning routine can set a positive tone for the rest of the day, helping you to stay focused and productive.

Finally, consistency helps manage setbacks. When we're consistent, we build resilience and learn to handle obstacles more effectively. It's easier to bounce back from failures because our regular efforts keep us grounded and focused on the bigger picture.

So, if you want to achieve long-term goals, remember that consistency is your best friend. It's the daily grind, the small steps, and the steady progress that lead to remarkable outcomes. Keep watering that garden, and you'll be amazed at the growth you'll see over time.

Strategies for Staying Motivated and Avoiding Burnout

You embark on a road trip toward your dream destination. The journey seems endless, fatigue sets in, and your initial enthusiasm fades. Then, you chance upon a convenient stop that revitalizes you and grants you a moment of respite. Energized and reinvigorated, you resume your journey, all set to conquer the remaining miles. That strategic break becomes the key to sustaining motivation and steering clear of burnout.

Here are some effective ways to keep your energy up and burnout at bay:

- **Set Clear and Achievable Goals:** Breaking big goals into smaller, manageable tasks can make them less daunting. Celebrate each small win along the way. This keeps the momentum going and makes the journey enjoyable.
- **Prioritize Self-Care:** It's crucial to take care of your mental and physical health. Make time for activities that recharge you, such as reading, walking, or spending time with loved ones. Regular breaks and enough sleep are essential to maintaining your energy levels.
- **Stay Organized:** Organizing your tasks and priorities can reduce stress. Use tools like to-do lists, planners, or digital apps to track your progress. This will help you stay on top of things and give you a sense of accomplishment as you tick off tasks.
- **Connect With Supportive People:** Surround yourself with people who motivate and support you. Share your goals with them and seek their encouragement. Sometimes, a quick chat with a friend or colleague can boost your motivation to keep going.
- **Mix Up Your Routine:** Monotony kills motivation. Introduce variety into your routine to keep things interesting. Try new ways of doing things, explore different environments, or learn new skills to stay engaged and motivated.
- **Reflect and Adjust:** Regularly reflect on your progress and adjust your strategies as needed. Understanding what works for you and what doesn't can help you stay motivated in the long run and avoid feeling overwhelmed.

- **Avoid Overcommitting:** Learn to say "no" to tasks or commitments that don't align with your priorities. Overloading yourself can quickly lead to burnout. Focus on what's most important and let go of the rest.

Overcoming Plateaus and Adapting to Challenges

Hitting a plateau can be incredibly frustrating. Whether you're working toward a personal goal, mastering a new skill, or making progress in your career, feeling stuck is a common experience. But don't worry, plateaus aren't the end of the road; they're just a part of the journey.

Here are some tips to help you overcome plateaus and adapt to challenges:

- **Change Your Approach:** Sometimes, breaking through a plateau means changing your tactics. If your current strategy isn't yielding results, try something new. This could be a different technique, a new angle, or a fresh perspective. For instance, if you're trying to learn a new language and find yourself stuck, switching to a new learning method or tool might reignite your progress.
- **Set Smaller, Specific Goals:** Large, vague goals can be overwhelming and lead to plateaus. Break your larger goal into smaller, specific tasks that are easier to manage and measure. This makes the overall objective seem more attainable and provides a sense of accomplishment with each completed step.
- **Seek Feedback:** Sometimes, an outside perspective is what you need to move forward. Don't hesitate to ask mentors, peers, or professionals for feedback. They can provide insights you might have overlooked and suggest new strategies to help you overcome your stagnation.
- **Take a Break:** At times, stepping away is the best way to overcome a plateau. Taking a break can help you recharge

and return with a fresh perspective. This doesn't mean giving up; it's about giving yourself the space to relax and clear your mind.

- **Stay Patient and Persistent:** Overcoming plateaus often requires patience and persistence. Remember that progress isn't always linear. There will be ups and downs, and staying committed to your goals is important, even during challenging times.

Reviewing and Adjusting Goals

Imagine you're on a road trip. You've mapped out your route, set your lunch, and ensured your vehicle is fit. But along the way, you'll likely encounter unexpected detours, breathtaking sights, and maybe even a flat tire. The journey toward achieving your goals is much like this trip. It's not always a straight path; sometimes, you need to pause, reflect, and adjust. This section is all about how to do just that—keeping your journey on track and your end goals in sight.

The Role of Reflection and Feedback in Goal Refinement

Reflection and feedback are like personal coaches for achieving your goals. They play vital roles in helping you grow, improve, and succeed.

Think of reflection as a mental pause button. It's when you take a step back to think about what you've done, how you did it, and what you learned from the experience. Reflection helps you understand your strengths and weaknesses, what worked well, and where you could do better next time. It's all about learning from your own experiences and using that knowledge to refine your approach.

Now, feedback is like a G.P.S. system giving you directions. It comes from others—like mentors, colleagues, or even customers—who share their observations and insights about your performance. Good feedback isn't just about pointing out mistakes; it's about highlighting what you're doing right and offering suggestions for improvement. It provides a different perspective you might not see, helping you course-correct and stay on track toward your goals.

Reflection and feedback form a powerful duo for goal refinement. When you reflect on your actions and decisions, you gain insights you can validate or expand upon with feedback. For example, you might reflect on a recent project and realize that your time management could improve. Feedback from your team might confirm this and offer strategies to improve.

Reflection and feedback offer several benefits crucial for personal and professional development. They support continuous improvement by facilitating ongoing learning and growth, allowing incremental enhancements over time. Additionally, these practices provide clarity and direction, helping you define clear objectives and align your efforts more effectively to achieve them personally.

Reflection and feedback foster self-awareness, resilience, and adaptability, essential traits for navigating challenges and evolving professionally. They also build strong relationships by promoting open communication, mutual understanding, trust, and collaboration among team members and stakeholders.

Techniques for Assessing Progress and Identifying Areas for Improvement

Have you ever felt like you're navigating a journey without a map? Understanding how to assess your progress and pinpoint areas for improvement can be like finding that compass—it keeps you on track toward your goals. Let's unlock some practical techniques that can help you track your progress and identify areas of improvement:

- **Performance Tracking:** Think of this as your scoreboard. Tracking your performance allows you to measure your achievements against your goals over time. This step keeps you informed and motivated, whether jotting down milestones or using sophisticated tools to monitor productivity.
- **Self-Assessment:** Take a moment to pause and reflect on your performance. Consider setting aside time to honestly evaluate your strengths and weaknesses. This will help you identify where you excel and where there's room for growth.
- **Feedback Loops:** Feedback is your secret weapon for growth. Create feedback loops by actively seeking input from mentors, peers, or colleagues. Their insights provide fresh perspectives and uncover blind spots you might have overlooked.
- **Goal Check-Ins:** Regularly revisit your goals to celebrate progress and adjust strategies as needed. Break big goals into smaller milestones to maintain momentum and stay focused on what matters most.
- **Analyzing Trends:** Look for patterns in your performance data. Identifying trends—like peak productivity times or recurring challenges—to refine your approach and optimize your efforts effectively.

Setting New Challenges and Pushing Beyond Comfort Zones

Ready to shake things up and go beyond the normal? Setting new challenges and stepping out of your comfort zone isn't just about achieving more—it's about discovering the superhero version of yourself.

I like to believe growth often starts where your cozy bubble ends. It could be signing up for that public speaking workshop when you're usually shy or taking on a project that's a bit out of your wheelhouse. Remember that time you learned to ride a bike? It was scary at first, but you felt unstoppable once you got the hang of it. That's the magic of pushing your limits!

Now, setting clear goals is like setting sail with a destination in mind. It's easier to steer when you know where you're headed. Whether aiming to master new software or lead a team project, breaking big goals into smaller, doable steps keeps you on track and less overwhelmed. It's like climbing a mountain—one step at a time gets you to the summit.

And you don't have to go alone! Surround yourself with cheer-leaders and mentors who've got your back. Their support makes all the difference. Whether it's friends, mentors, or even online communities, having people in your corner helps you stay moti-vated and bounce back stronger when things get challenging.

Speaking of challenges, setbacks are part of the adventure. Have you ever tried baking a cake and ended up with something that looked more like a pancake? It happens! Instead of getting discour-aged, think of it as a learning experience. Adapting and bouncing back from setbacks builds resilience and makes you even more capable in the long run.

So, embrace the thrill of stepping into the unknown and surprising yourself. Setting new challenges and pushing beyond comfort zones isn't just about reaching goals; it's about discovering your superpowers and becoming the best version of yourself. Stay curi-ous, stay resilient, and keep exploring. Your next adventure awaits!

KEY TAKEAWAYS

- After achieving initial success, it's crucial to keep the momentum going. Develop a routine and maintain consistent actions to ensure long-term success. Strategies to stay motivated include setting clear goals, prioritizing self-care, staying organized, connecting with supportive people, varying your routine, reflecting regularly, and avoiding over-commitment.

- Consistency is essential for long-term success. Regular, repeated actions lead to steady progress and significant achievements over time. It helps develop habits, boosts confidence, and builds resilience, making it easier to manage setbacks and stay focused on your goals.
- Plateaus are a natural part of the journey to success. To overcome them, change your approach, set smaller specific goals, seek feedback, take breaks, and stay patient. Regularly reviewing and adjusting your goals helps you stay on track despite unexpected challenges.

Our journey to self-discipline is coming to an end; it's clear that sustaining long-term success is a continuous adventure. Just like running a marathon, the exhilaration of crossing the finish line is only the beginning. Remember, success isn't a one-time event but a series of small, consistent steps that build over time. It's about staying motivated, reflecting on your progress, and being flexible enough to adjust your plans when life throws you a curveball.

CONCLUSION

You are the master of your destiny. You can influence, direct, and control your own environment. You can make your life what you want it to be.

NAPOLEON HILL

As we reach the end of our journey together, we must reflect on the powerful tools and insights we've uncovered. Self-discipline isn't just a skill; it's a transformative force that can reshape your life. Let's revisit the key takeaways that can propel you toward a more disciplined future filled with success and fulfillment.

First and foremost, self-discipline is the bedrock of all achievement. It's what sets the stage for lasting success, going beyond motivation to foster a deep, enduring commitment to your goals. We've discussed the science behind self-discipline, exploring how understanding your brain's role in self-control and embracing delayed gratification can steer you toward better decisions and a more focused life.

Clear goals are your roadmap to success. By setting specific, actionable objectives and breaking them down into manageable tasks, you create a clear path forward. This clarity allows you to prioritize effectively, tackle obstacles head-on, and stay on track with the support of accountability partners and useful tools.

Time management is another secret weapon. Mastering your schedule through prioritization, structured routines, and productivity techniques like the Pomodoro Technique can help you make the most of every moment. This disciplined approach to time allows you to balance work, leisure, and self-care, ensuring a well-rounded and fulfilling life.

Don't forget that self-control is a muscle that strengthens the more you build it. By understanding your impulses, practicing mindfulness, and building healthy habits, you can develop greater self-control. This resilience will help you stay focused on your goals, even when faced with temptation or distraction.

Self-compassion acts as your ally. To cultivate a compassionate and resilient mindset, it's vital to dispel perfectionism myths, prioritize self-care, and conquer patterns of self-sabotage. Embracing self-compassion empowers you to bounce back from challenges and continually progress with optimism.

Willpower can be cultivated and replenished. Recognizing when your willpower is depleted and restoring it are key skills. Building willpower reserves, setting boundaries, and using temptation bundling and reward systems can reinforce your self-discipline and keep you on track.

Overcoming procrastination is a game-changer. By understanding the roots of procrastination and implementing practical strategies to beat it, you can transform your approach to tasks. Breaking tasks into smaller steps, utilizing time-blocking, and maintaining a mindset that values progress over perfection are essential strategies.

Long-term success is about consistency and adaptability. Maintaining momentum through consistent effort, reflecting on your progress, and adjusting your goals as needed ensure that you continue to grow and achieve. Embrace new challenges and push beyond your comfort zone to unlock your full potential.

Now that you have these powerful tools and insights at your disposal, it's time to take action. Commit to implementing at least one strategy from this book daily for the next 10 days. Transformation is within your grasp, and every small step brings you closer to your goals. Embrace this journey wholeheartedly.

Remember, success isn't a distant destination but a series of small, consistent actions. Each day is a new opportunity to reinforce your self-discipline and move closer to your dreams. Your future self will thank you for the dedication and perseverance you show today. Keep pushing forward, stay committed, and never underestimate the power of your efforts. You have the potential to create a life of success, fulfillment, and happiness. I challenge you to believe in yourself, take action, and let your journey to mastering self-discipline begin today.

Thank you so much for purchasing my book.

You could have picked from dozens of other books, and I'm incredibly grateful for your purchase of my book. It means the world to me that you chose my book out of many options available to you. Thank you for taking the time to read it all the way through. Before you leave, I would like to kindly ask for a small favor. Would you consider leaving a review on the platform? Your review would tremendously support independent authors like myself. Your feedback will help me continue writing books that cater to your needs and preferences.

I would deeply appreciate hearing from you.

>> Leave a review on Amazon US <<
>> Leave a review on Amazon UK <<

BIBLIOGRAPHY

Agbaje, A. (2024, March 3). *Celebrating milestones: fueling your journey to success.* https://www.linkedin.com/pulse/celebrating-milestones-fueling-your-jour ney-success-adekunle-agbaje-b8ktf?trk=public_post_main-feed-card_feed-arti cle-content

Alimov, F. (2024, May 10). *Embrace the struggle: why stepping out of your comfort zone is essential.* https://www.linkedin.com/pulse/embrace-struggle-why-stepping-out-your-comfort-zone-essential-alimov-hhiyc

American Psychological Association. (2012). *What you need to know about willpower: the psychological science of self-control.* https://www.apa.org/topics/personality/willpower

Angadia, O. (2023, February 1). *Avoid burnout and stay motivated - tips and strategies.* https://cubo.to/blog/avoid-burnout-and-stay-motivated-tips-and-strategies

Annual review: cracking the code: mastering your annual performance review. (2024, April 6). FasterCapital. https://fastercapital.com/content/Annual-reviewCracking-the-Code--Mastering-Your-Annual-Performance-Review.html#Identifying-Areas-of-Improvement-and-Development.html

Arnsten, A., Mazure, C. M., & Sinha, R. (2012). This is your brain in meltdown. *Scientific American, 306*(4), 48–53. https://doi.org/10.1038/scientificameri can0412-48

Asana. (2021, January 21). *Overcome analysis paralysis with these 4 tips.* Asana. https://asana.com/resources/analysis paralysis

Bastein, B. (2022, March 18). *What is the difference between self-discipline and motivation?* Bachir Bastien. https://bachirbastien.com/2022/03/18/what-is-the-differ ence-between-self-discipline-and-motivation/

Bastos, F. (2024a, March 8). *Understanding the psychology behind instant gratification(+ examples).* https://mindowl.org/the-psychology-behind-instant-gratification-with-examples/#:~:text=Instant%20Gratification%20Theory%20explains%20why

Berkman, E. T., Graham, A. M., & Fisher, P. A. (2012). Training self-control: a domain-general translational neuroscience approach. *Child Development Perspectives*, n/a-n/a. https://doi.org/10.1111/j.1750-8606.2012.00248.x

Białaszek, W., Gaik, M., McGoun, E., & Zielonka, P. (2015). Impulsive people have a compulsion for immediate gratification—certain or uncertain. *Frontiers in Psychology, 6*(515). https://doi.org/10.3389/fpsyg.2015.00515

Biola. (2013, March 7). *Neuroplasticity and self-control.* Biola University Center for Christian Thought / The Table. https://cct.biola.edu/neuroplasticity-and-self-control/

Boogaard, K. (2023, December 26). *How to write SMART goals.* Atlassian. https://www.atlassian.com/blog/productivity/how-to-write-smart-goals

Bradford, A. (2023, February 28). *Task management tips: How to break down work projects.* Understood. https://www.understood.org/en/articles/task-management-at-work-break-down-projects

Break the cycle of procrastination. (n.d.). Learning Strategies Center. https://lsc.cornell.edu/break-the-cycle-of-procrastination/

Breaking down your goals into actionable steps | Wendaful Planning. (2017, December 8). Wendaful. https://www.wendaful.com/2017/12/breaking-down-goals/

Breaking down your tasks into manageable pieces. (n.d.). https://www.workiro.com/blog/how-to-break-down-tasks-into-manageable-pieces

Burke, K. (2020, September 1). *Why you need clarity and vision to reach your goals.* Kristin Burke. https://kristinburke.com/why-you-need-clarity-and-vision-to-reach-your-goals/

Celebrating milestones and progress along the way. (2024, April 1). FasterCapital. https://fastercapital.com/topics/celebrating-milestones-and-progress-along-the-way.html#:~:text=Celebrating%20milestones%20and%20progress%20is%20a%20crucial%20part%20of%20achieving

Celebrating your milestones: Unlocking the motivational power of progress. (2023, June 30). WindowStill. https://www.windowstill.com/celebrating-your-milestones-unlocking-the-motivational-power-of-progress/posts/

CFI team. (2022). *SMART goals.* Corporate Finance Institute; CFI. https://corporatefinanceinstitute.com/resources/management/smart-goal/

Chandra, P. (2023, October 9). *The role of the environment in building self-discipline.* Let's Go Creative. https://pooranchandra.substack.com/p/the-role-of-the-environment-in-building

Cherry, K. (2019). *Can you resist temptation with delayed gratification?* Verywell Mind. https://www.verywellmind.com/delayed-gratification-why-wait-for-what-you-want-2795429

Cole, M. (2024, March 1). *Powerful principles of goal setting for effective goals.* Self Determined Life. https://selfdeterminedlife.com/goal-setting-criticism/

Conti, R. (2019). *Delay of gratification | Psychology.* Encyclopædia Britannica. https://www.britannica.com/science/delay-of-gratification#ref1206154

Dee, M. (2017, June 29). *Dispelling the myths about perfectionists.* Embracing the Unexpected. https://www.embracingtheunexpected.com/dispelling-myths-about-perfectionists/

Diekelmann, S. (2014). Sleep for cognitive enhancement. *Frontiers in Systems Neuroscience, 8*(46). https://doi.org/10.3389/fnsys.2014.00046

Eatough, E. (2022, October 11). *7 ways to overcome fear of failure and move forward in life.* https://www.betterup.com/blog/how-to-overcome-fear-of-failure

Ego depletion: The more decisions you make, the worse they become! | Welcome to the Jungle. (2024, March 27). Welcome to the Jungle. https://www.welcometothejungle.com/en/articles/ego-depletion-decision-fatigue

Eleven common obstacles to achieving goals with strategies. (2024, January 28).

Elevationvibe.com. https://elevationvibe.com/blog/obstacles-to-achieving-goals/

Explain the role of feedback in refining and achieving objectives. | *TutorChase.* (n.d.). Www.tutorchase.com. Retrieved June 11, 2024, from https://www.tutorchase.com/answers/ib/business-management/explain-the-role-of-feedback-in-refining-and-achieving-objectives

FAQ: How can you break down large goals into smaller, more manageable steps? (n.d.). Www.everyday.design. https://www.everyday.design/faqs/how-can-you-break-down-large-goals-into-smaller-more-manageable-steps

FAQ: How do you celebrate achieving your goals? (n.d.). Www.everyday.design. Retrieved June 6, 2024, from https://www.everyday.design/faqs/how-do-you-celebrate-achieving-your-goals

Finding inspiration in role models and success stories. (2024, April 1). FasterCapital. https://fastercapital.com/topics/finding-inspiration-in-role-models-and-success-stories.html

Goldstein, T. (2024, February 9). *Mastering self-discipline for personal and professional growth.* https://www.linkedin.com/pulse/mastering-self-discipline-personal-professional-growth-tom-goldstein-qz0ff

Greene, J. (2023, October 2). *How to prioritize when everything feels important.* https://zapier.com/blog/how-to-prioritize/

Hanke, S. (2018, August 18). *Council Post: Three steps to overcoming resistance.* Forbes. https://www.forbes.com/sites/forbescoachescouncil/2018/08/14/three-steps-to-overcoming-resistance/?sh=4d1600e15eae

Hare, T. A., Camerer, C. F., & Rangel, A. (2009). Self-control in decision-making involves modulation of the vmPFC valuation system. *Science, 324*(5927), 646–648. https://doi.org/10.1126/science.1168450

Health, I. (2021, April 16). *Why it's important to allow yourself to rest.* https://integrishealth.org/resources/on-your-health/2021/april/why-its-important-to-allow-yourself-to-rest

Herrity, J. (2023, July 10). *How to write SMART goals (with examples).* Indeed. https://www.indeed.com/career-advice/career-development/how-to-write-smart-goals

Hollinshead, J. (2024, May 15). *Blog - Self-discipline vs. self-compassion* | Peak Resilience. https://www.peak-resilience.com/blog/self-discipline-vs-self-compassion

Holly, H. C. (2024, June 2). *Overcoming 10 common barriers to achieving your personal goals.* https://theintentionhabit.com/barriers-to-achieving-goals/

House, T. G. (2022, April 4). *Focusing on self-control with mindfulness* | The Guest House. Www.theguesthouseocala.com. https://www.theguesthouseocala.com/focusing-on-self-control-with-mindfulness/

How can you identify and eliminate time-wasting activities in your workday? (2023, September 20). https://www.linkedin.com/advice/0/how-can-you-identify-eliminate-time-wasting-activities-1c

How to overcome self-doubt when achieving your goals. (2020, December 14). https://

www.linkedin.com/pulse/how-overcome-self-doubt-when-achieving-your-goals-rory

The importance of goal clarity and specificity. (2024, April 4). FasterCapital. https://fastercapital.com/topics/the-importance-of-goal-clarity-and-specificity.html

Indeed editorial team. (2022, June 25). *How to measure your progress effectively in 5 steps.* Indeed Career Guide. https://www.indeed.com/career-advice/career-development/measure-progress

Loli, C. (2023, October 23). *Identifying areas for improvement: A comprehensive guide for performance management and measurement.* https://www.boostmavens.com/performance-tracking-and-analysis-identifying-areas-for-improvement

Jacox, C. (2018, June 19). *What is the difference between motivation and discipline?* https://www.linkedin.com/pulse/what-difference-between-motivation-discipline-casey-jacox

Kaffman, J. (n.d.). *Willpower depletion.* Retrieved June 10, 2024, from https://personalmba.com/willpower-depletion/

Life, C. (2017, April 26). *How to deal with obstacles to stay on track toward your goals* | AIU. https://www.aiuniv.edu/blog/2017/april/how-to-deal-with-obstacles-to-stay-on-track-toward-your-goals

Lifecoachtraining. (2023, July 12). *Overcoming procrastination: Motivation and goal setting strategies.* Life Coach Certification Online. https://lifecoachtraining.co/overcoming-procrastination-motivation-and-goal-setting-strategies/

Locke, E. A., Shaw, K. N., Saari, L. M., & Latham, G. P. (1981). Goal setting and task performance: 1969-1980. *Psychological Bulletin, 90*(1), 125–152. MA, C. E. A. (2018, June 19). What is instant gratification? (Definition & examples). https://positivepsychology.com/instant-gratification/#instant-gratifications-effect-on-society

Makshyna, D. (2020, October 20). *From dreams to results: The power of goal setting.* The Female Factor. https://www.femalefactor.global/post/from-dreams-to-results-the-power-of-goal-setting

Marinoff, E. (2019, July 8). *Why is internal motivation so powerful (and how to find it).* Lifehack. https://www.lifehack.org/839224/internal-motivation

Martin, D. S. (2019, April 16). *The truth about perfectionism: Dispelling 6 myths about perfectionism.* Live Well with Sharon Martin. https://www.livewellwithsharonmartin.com/perfectionism-myths-and-truths/

Mclachlan, S. (2021, December 22). *The science of habit: How to rewire your brain.* Healthline. https://www.healthline.com/health/the-science-of-habit#4

Mind Tools Content Team. (2023). *How to stop procrastinating.* https://www.mindtools.com/a5plzk8/how-to-stop-procrastinating

Nauma, E. (2014, March 24). *How does mindfulness improve self-control?* Greater Good. https://greatergood.berkeley.edu/article/item/How_does_mindfulness_help_control_behavior#:~:text=By%20paying%20attention%20to%20way

Neff, K. D. (2009). The role of self-compassion in development: A healthier way to relate to oneself. *Human Development, 52*(4), 211–214. https://doi.org/10.1159/000215071

Newman, L. (2017, August 28). *Dispelling the myths about perfectionists guest post by Maree Dee* | Journey to Imperfect. https://www.journeytoimperfect.com/2017/08/28/dispelling-myths-perfectionists-guest-maree-dee/

Nine tips for setting healthy boundaries. (2020, July 30). Calm Blog. https://www.calm.com/blog/9-tips-for-setting-healthy-boundaries

Overcoming fear of failure - Everything you need to know. (2023, September 13). Calmer You. https://www.calmer-you.com/fear-of-failure/#:~:text=Adopting%20a%20growth%20mindset&text=This%20involves%20taking%20on%20challenges

Pattemore, C. (2021, June 3). *10 ways to build and preserve better boundaries.* Psych Central. https://psychcentral.com/lib/10-way-to-build-and-preserve-better-boundaries

Peak, S. (2024, May 14). *Best tools for setting and tracking goals.* https://www.business.com/articles/11-best-tools-for-setting-and-tracking-goals/

Pignatiello, G. A., Martin, R. J., & Hickman, R. L. (2018). Decision fatigue: A conceptual analysis. *Journal of Health Psychology, 25*(1), 135910531876351. https://doi.org/10.1177/1359105318763510

Повар, 6 I. F. P. Y. H. Q.-Д. (2021, April 26). *7 common obstacles to your goals and how to navigate them.* Rainmakers. https://gorainmakers.com/2021/04/26/7-common-obstacles-to-your-goals-and-how-to-navigate-them/

The power of goal setting: How to create and achieve meaningful goals. (2023, April 29). https://www.linkedin.com/pulse/power-goal-setting-how-create-achieve-meaningful-goals-adila-ismail

Ragland, L. (2020, November 24). *Ways to manage stress.* WebMD. https://www.webmd.com/balance/stress-management/stress-management

Raypole, C. (2020, April 27). *Here's how to beat indecision.* Healthline. https://www.healthline.com/health/mental-health/analysis-paralysis

Relax! On the invaluable role of rest and regeneration. (n.d.). Oakywood.shop. Retrieved June 9, 2024, from https://oakywood.shop/blogs/news/relax-rest-and-regeneration

Robbins, T. (n.d.). *Delayed gratification: Importance, FAQs & more.* https://www.tonyrobbins.com/achieve-lasting-weight-loss/delayed-gratification/

Robinson, L., & Smith, M. (2023, October 11). *Stress management.* HelpGuide. https://www.helpguide.org/articles/stress/stress-management.htm

Robinson, R. (2024, April 3). *Analysis paralysis: How to make decisions & move forward.* RyRob.com: A blog by Ryan Robinson | Learn how to blog and make money on the internet. https://www.ryrob.com/analysis-paralysis/

Rohani, B. (2024, May 14). *Goal setting and achievement: Roadmap to success.* https://www.linkedin.com/pulse/goal-setting-achievement-roadmap-success-beth-rohani-qudyc?trk=public_post

The role of accountability and support. (2024, April 5). FasterCapital. https://fastercapital.com/topics/the-role-of-accountability-and-support.html

The role of feedback and self-reflection in enhancing productivity and performance. (2023,

August 26). Zeotalentssolutions. https://zoetalentsolutions.com/the-role-of-feedback-and-self-reflection-in-enhancing-productivity-and-performance/

The role of rest and relaxation in work success. (2024, April 6). FasterCapital. https://fastercapital.com/topics/the-role-of-rest-and-relaxation-in-work-success.html

Ryan, F. (2016, March 26). *10 ways to support your willpower.* Dummies. https://www.dummies.com/article/body-mind-spirit/emotional-health-psychology/emotional-health/willpower/10-ways-to-support-your-willpower-151697/

Sable. (2016). *What do you actually do to replenish your willpower?* https://www.lesswrong.com/posts/nRdioePkHTjsNmd87/what-do-you-actually-do-to-replenish-your-willpower

Saleh, J. (2023, October 30). *Prioritization and decision making: How to make the right business choices.* Monitask. https://www.monitask.com/en/blog/prioritization-and-decision-making-how-to-make-the-right-business-choices#Tips_for_Prioritizing_Projects

Sasson, R. (2023, February 16). *Why rest is important for health, productivity and happiness.* https://www.successconsciousness.com/blog/wellness/rest-and-relaxation-are-important/

Self-discipline benefits and is important in your life. (2023, February 21). Aeologic Blog. https://www.aeologic.com/blog/self-discipline-benefits-and-its-importance-in-your-life/

Shah, S. (2022, December 11). Self-*discipline benefits and its importance in your life.* https://www.linkedin.com/pulse/self-discipline-benefits-its-importance-your-life-salar-shah

Snee, T. (2016, June 6). *This is your brain - no self-control.* The University of Iowa. https://now.uiowa.edu/news/2012/06/your-brain-no-self-control

Staff, F. (2024, January 26). *The art of strategy prioritization: Overview, benefits, and guide.* As We May Think — Products & Tools for Thought. https://fibery.io/blog/product-management/strategy-prioritization/

Staff, T. (2018, May 12). Self-*discipline: Its benefits and importance (Sport & life).* Triathlon LAB. https://triathlonlab.com/blogs/news/self-discipline-its-benefits-and-importance-sport-life

Sutton, J. (2018, February 23). *10 techniques to manage stress & 13 quick tips.* https://positivepsychology.com/stress-management-techniques-tips-burn-out/

T, M. (2024, June 3). *3 tips to eliminate time wasters and distractions.* https://www.linkedin.com/pulse/3-tips-eliminate-time-wasters-distractions-matthias-trvly-xknqc

Team, I. E. (2022, May 25). *9 common workplace time-wasters and how to avoid them.* Indeed Career Guide. https://www.indeed.com/career-advice/career-development/time-wasters-and-how-to-avoid-them

Techniques and tips for managing negative emotions. (n.d.). Retrieved June 8, 2024, from https://www.vinmec.com/en/news/health-news/healthy-lifestyle/techniques-and-tips-for-managing-negative-emotions/

Try this simple trick to overcome procrastination. (2024, March 2). Psychology Today.

https://www.psychologytoday.com/intl/blog/liking-the-child-you-love/202402/try-this-simple-trick-to-overcome-procrastination

Waite, R. (2024, May 14). *Overcoming self-doubt, lack of motivation and procrastination.* https://www.robinwaite.com/blog/how-to-overcome-self-doubt-lack-of-motivation-and-procrastination

Waller, J. (2021, April 8). *How to eliminate time-wasting activities at work.* https://www.findmyshift.com/blog/how-to-eliminate-time-wasting-activities-at-work#:~:text=Cut%20your%20notifications

What is the difference between self-discipline and motivation? (n.d.). MTNTOUGH. Retrieved May 31, 2024, from https://mtntough.com/blogs/mtntough-blog/self-discipline-vs-motivation

Wooll, M. (2022, February 24). *A quick guide to develop discipline – How to be disciplined.* https://www.betterup.com/blog/how-to-be-disciplined

World, P. (2023, July 31). *The importance of consistency in personal growth.* Psychology Magazine. https://www.psychologs.com/the-importance-of-consistency-in-personal-growth/?amp=1

Made in the USA
Middletown, DE
09 December 2024